Talking Stones

by

LIONEL FANTHORPE AND RICHARD PAWELKO

And based upon the ITV1 Wales television series produced by Zip Tv.

First Impression – 2003

ISBN 1 84323 200 6

Printed in Wales by
Gomer Press, Llandysul, Ceredigion

Contents

Chapter One

A Grave Introduction

Graveyards are fascinating places, not only because our ancestors rest there, but also because they form a directory of stones, an index to interesting lives gone by. Cemeteries are solemn pageants of the past – and constant reminders to us, the living, to make the most of our time on Earth. Like Kipling, they advise us ominously to 'fill the unforgiving minute with sixty seconds' worth of distance run'.

Co-author Lionel Fanthorpe examines a seventeenth-century table tomb.

Many stones display epitaphs with stories to tell. Such graves are passports to the past, our letters of introduction to the people who lived and died here. Some are engraved with curious riddles and enigmas; others bear tales of heroism or tragedy. Impressive memorials commemorate the great and the good. Other stones remind us of interesting – or unusual – men, women and even animals. But whatever their message or design, all these stones connect us with the realities of yesterday's people.

The very earliest British grave markers carried no inscriptions. They were just standing stones, or simple structures to contain and guard the body, usually that of a leader or chieftain. The cromlech at Pentre Ifan near Nevern in West Wales is typical of these bleak, primeval memorials.

The first memorials with accessible inscriptions date from 2000 years ago, taking us back to Roman times and the earliest Latin alphabet. But what we would readily recognise as churchyards didn't appear until the eighth century AD. This was when the concept of 'God's Acre', a sacred burial ground, was developed, and it was in places like this that we found many of our stories and mysteries.

According to tradition, it was during the seventh century that St Cuthbert of Lindisfarne was granted permission by the Pope to establish graveyards around holy places. This was intended to remind the living of their own mortality, and to ensure that Masses were said for the local dead to speed their passage through Purgatory. At this stage, however, the graves of ordinary people were rarely, if ever, marked. Their bodies, wrapped in linen shrouds, were usually lowered into the ground without any other protection. Inevitably, as the years passed, more bodies would be lowered on top of previous interments. In many old churchyards, we might see only 100 or so gravestones, but with an average of ten burials a year, a churchyard which has been in use for 800 years – and many have – contains at least 8000 bodies. And that is why the ground looks so uneven.

Recumbent Knight at St Nicholas's, Montgomery.

Inside church buildings, the earliest tombs containing bodies date from the twelfth century and usually cover the remains of church dignitaries such as Bishops. By the thirteenth century, however, the laity started to get a look-in, so that the recumbent effigy of a knight, or the local Lord of the Manor with his Lady, would be installed among the church hierarchy. A century later, finely carved stone canopies were erected over these reclining figures of the gentry, thus providing a valuable source of income to country craftsmen. Memorials, therefore, were almost exclusively the preserve of the wealthy – mainly big landowners – during the Middle Ages, while outside the churches, the ground level was slowly but inevitably rising to accommodate the vast majority of the people.

Canopy tomb at St Nicholas's, Montgomery.

During Elizabethan times, money became more equitably distributed, and this created a middle class who could afford the luxury of personal memorials and grave-markers. It was during this period that overcrowded church tombs and crypts began to generate such a foul stench of corruption and decay that the upper classes now preferred to bury their dead in the adjacent graveyards outside the churches – even if that meant their loved ones lying alongside the commoners.

Sheep were then of prime importance economically, and commercial interests were powerful enough to influence burial practices. By 1670, an Act of Parliament ordained that the dead should be buried in woollen stuff – flannel. This had to be white, but the quality, like the prices, catered for people of every age and income level. Wrapped in their woollen shrouds, the dead might well be conveyed from their homes to the church in a communal Parish coffin, which would then be emptied out at the graveside and stored in the church ready for its next passenger.

From the 1700s onwards, inscriptions on stones became more verbose. Epitaphs emphasised the frailty of human life and its continuity beyond the grave. These memorials provide modern investigators with valuable clues to the way that previous generations lived and what they believed in, as we will see later on in this book.

By the mid-nineteenth century, the problem of inadequate churchyards forced Parliament to pass the Burial Act of 1852, creating licensed cemeteries. These became the responsibility of Local Authorities in much the same way as drains and water supplies, which were constructed, extended and managed to meet the needs of growing urban populations.

Nowadays, when 80% of human remains are cremated, burial problems have been alleviated, but, sadly, the grand old traditions of graveyard sculpture and epitaph writing seem to be declining proportionately. Future generations of investigators may well find that these intriguing stone messages from the past are growing rarer.

At night, graveyards seem to be very different places. In the dark, they can arouse feelings of unease, dread of supernatural happenings and even the fear of ghosts rising from the dead. This is the time and place when our imaginations can be at their most fertile and vivid. To our ancestors, death was the ultimate mystery, wrapped in timeless superstition and strange rituals. Some of their attitude still lingers among the shadows of a midnight graveyard.

> 'T is now the very witching time of night
> When churchyards yawn and hell itself breathes out
> Contagion to this world.
> (*Hamlet*, Act III, Scene 2)

This Shakespearean awareness of death – with all its philosophical, psychological and sociological implications – bridges the gulf between the pragmatic facts of simply disposing of the dead with a mixture of dignity, and hygienic efficiency, and investigating the real metaphysical *meaning* of death.

On November 13th, 1789, Benjamin Franklin wrote in a letter to Jean-Baptiste Le Roy that the only certainties in life were death and taxes. The way modern medicine is advancing, taxes may soon be the only certainty: genetic engineering, cloning, spare-part surgery and cryogenics are already postponing death. It may eventually become obsolete, but until it does, graveyards, tombs and epitaphs will continue to exert their strange spells over us.

There are cultures in which passing those milestones of time and moving on to achieve the status of ancestor is calmly regarded as just one more rite of passage: like birth, puberty, adulthood, parenthood and retirement. There are communities who bring out the remains of their dead on special festive occasions and chat unconcernedly to their bones, as if their ancestors were still as active and participative as the living members of the family.

Chief Seattle – after whom the great American Pacific Coast city is named –

The bleak, isolated cholera cemetery at Cefn Golau, Tredegar.

was Chief of the Suquamish Nation when the 1855 treaty was drawn up. It restricted his people to reservations and conveyed the rest of their ancestral lands to the new settlers. As part of his formal acceptance speech, the wise old Chief said:

> The very dust under your feet responds more lovingly to our footsteps than to yours, because it is the ashes of our ancestors . . . the soil is rich with the life of our kindred.
> To us the ashes of our ancestors are sacred and their final resting-place is hallowed ground.
> The dead are not powerless. Dead – did I say? There is no death: only a change of worlds.

This North American idea of the lingering power of dead ancestors within their burial soil is surprisingly close to Celtic ideas. The death of an ancestor was regarded as a very important event: so it became essential to ascertain that death really was death – not just a very deep sleep or coma from which the person would recover and resume life on Earth.

Once death had been established beyond the faintest shadow of doubt, it had to be faced with traditional Celtic courage. We are the only living creature who knows it is going to die. The brilliant old Marquis of Rochefoucauld-Liancourt understood that only too well when he wrote:

Death is like the sun: no one can stare at it for very long.

Lionel beside the statue of unsurpassable Welsh runner Guto Nyth Brân.

Chapter Two

Symbols in Cemeteries

The most effective epitaphs can convey their messages through symbols in a kind of pictorial shorthand.

ANCHOR

The anchor was an early Christian symbol for hope – 'Will your anchor hold in the storms of life?' Many of Christ's earliest disciples were fishermen like Peter, who knew all about the storms on the Sea of Galilee. The anchor signifies stability, holding on against all difficulties, and resistance to life's gales, tides and storms. It also means that like a ship that anchors in different ports, we experience the changing scenes of life. The anchor was also used as an assay mark on precious metals. In some minds, the anchor can also signify a final resting-place.

ANGEL

In the Bible, we have only a few names of angels, such as Gabriel and St Michael the Archangel. However, it records that angels of the Lord were sent as messengers to Abraham, to Lot, to Zachariah, and to the Virgin Mary. In one instance in the Old Testament, a couple asked the name of an angel and were told that his name was secret. Various orders and ranks of angels such as the *cherubim* and the *seraphim* are noted. They are thought to be the guides who lead the souls of the dead to Paradise.

ARK

The Ark symbolises safety and protection. The Ark of Moses saved the infant when it was left among the Nile's bulrushes. The Ark of the Covenant symbolised God's presence with the Israelites, after Moses led them out of Egypt. The floating Ark of Noah preserved a man, his family, and the animals. So the graveyard Ark symbolises safe passage from Earth to Heaven.

BEEHIVE/BEE

The bee is a symbol of hard work: we speak of a hive of industry. It creates sweetness and is a store of sweetness. Bees were a popular symbol in Renaissance Italy and they were used mysteriously as symbols in part of the Rennes-le-Château mystery. They also feature prominently in the symbolism of ancient Crete. The idea may perhaps be that the life of Heaven is like the communal life of the hive. The bee symbol in Welsh graveyards indicates a long life well spent in useful activities, and the hope of the sweetness of Heaven as a fitting reward.

BED

This is a symbol of death, sleep, repose, or an earthly ending. A bed is also thought of in the sense of a bed of soil, like a flower bed. When the sleep image is pursued, the bed can be seen as a symbol of waking again after death, in a promise of resurrection.

BOOK

Scrolls existed before the codex form we recognise as a book. The word Bible (*Biblos*) means book, so we have The Holy Bible – the holy book. The cemetery symbolism refers to God's Book of Life where the names of the faithful who will enjoy eternal life have all been entered.

BUTTERFLY

The butterfly, emerging from the pupa, and soaring upwards with a new body, represents resurrection.

CIRCLE

An unbroken line comes to mean 'eternity'. The symbol of the circle reminds us of immortality.

COLUMN

A column, or pillar, signifies strength and the ability to carry a load. The symbol of the broken pillar, often found in churchyards, indicates the loss of a strong and loving companion who shared life's load.

CROSS

This is the ultimate Christian symbol of eternal life. The empty cross signifies Christ's triumphant resurrection. It proclaims that Death has no power over Him or his followers.

CROWN

St Stephen was the first Christian martyr, and martyrs were said to have achieved the 'crown of life'. The crown symbol in graveyards suggests that an imperishable and glorious crown awaits the Christian soul in Paradise.

DOVE

This is the symbol of innocence, purity and peace.

GATES

This symbolises entry into Heaven via the gates of gold and the gates of pearl. Loved ones who have passed over before us are said to be waiting to welcome us at the Heavenly Gates.

HANDS

Clasped hands are frequently seen as symbols in churchyards and signify both the sadness of parting and the prospect of joyful reunion.

HEART

This is the symbol of trust, love, courage and faithful devotion.

HOLLY

The Holly represented Christ's passion: the red berries were blood; the spines on the leaves symbolised the crown of thorns.

HORSES

These symbolise the Four Horsemen of the Apocalypse as a reminder of the end of the world and the Second Coming of Christ. Horses also symbolised strength and speed, and therefore a swift passage from Earth to Paradise.

HOURGLASS

This symbolised the sands of time where the certainty of an end reminds us of the finite nature of human life.

IVY

Ivy can embody the sincerity and faithfulness, and the immortality and friendship that clings so tightly that it transcends Death.

I.H.S.

These are the first three letters (*iota*, *eta* and *sigma*) from the start of the Greek spelling of Jesus. Sometimes interpreted as Jesus Christ, Saviour, or In His Service.

LABYRINTH

A maze or labyrinth signifies life's difficult and confusing pathways, beyond which Heaven can eventually be reached.

LAMB

This signifies purity and innocence, and is often used as a symbol on a child's grave. Jesus himself was the Lamb of God, to whom all children are especially precious.

LAUREL

Originally, this was the wreath or chaplet for victors at Greek and Roman Games. The spiritual symbolism is victory over sin.

LILY

Lilies symbolise purity. They can also mean death, the ultimate purification, after which the redeemed and forgiven soul progresses to Heaven.

LION

A lion symbolises strength, courage, leadership, power, and ultimately kingship. St. Mark's symbol is a winged lion. The lion in a graveyard indicates that Christ, the Lion of God, will guard the Christian soul on its journey to Heaven.

OBELISK

This is the symbol of power and ownership; it also symbolises the Christianization of the Egyptian Sun-god.

OLIVE BRANCH

This is the symbol of peace, signifying that the departed soul has made its everlasting peace with God, and now resides with Him in Heaven.

PALM

This symbol reminds us of Christ's triumphal entry into Jerusalem, which in turn represents the Christian soul's joyful entry into Heaven after earthly death.

PASSION-FLOWER

The Passion-Flower represents the Holy Trinity – Father, Son and Holy Spirit. It also symbolises the crown of thorns which Christ wore so that his redeemed followers could achieve a crown of eternal life.

PEACOCK

Originally this bird was sacred to the Roman goddess Juno, and her Greek equivalent, Hera. She put the eyes of her watchman, Argos, into the bird's tail when he was slain in his sleep by Hercules after Orpheus had played his lyre. In the churchyard it symbolises the eyes of God and the angels, constantly watching over the Christian soul to ensure its safe arrival in Heaven. It also reminds Christians to be constantly vigilant against temptation and sin.

PELICAN

The idea that it pierced its breast to feed its young may have come from people watching the young feed from the parents' huge bills and thinking they were actually feeding from the breast. It symbolises the sacrament of the Mass where Christ metaphorically feeds his disciples with his own body, and gives them his blood to drink. In graveyards it signifies that those who partake of Christ's sacred body and blood achieve eternal and abundant life.

PHOENIX

The Phoenix of mythology rises from the ashes of its own funeral pyre. It symbolises new life after death.

PILLOW

A pillow symbolises the sleep of death, after which the believer wakes to eternal life in Paradise.

ROCKS

They symbolise the unwavering steadfastness of Christian faith. Simon became Peter the rock, on which the Church was founded.

ROPE

A rope is an emblem of helpfulness, as when throwing a rope to a drowning man, or using a rope to scale a dangerous cliff safely. It symbolises the rope of life which God throws to all who ask for his help.

SCYTHE/SICKLE

These symbolise the idea of cutting, harvesting, or the completion of a process. Father Time is portrayed as carrying a scythe, which eventually severs our earthly lives. Death is portrayed as the grim reaper. So is the Angel of Death.

SHELL

The symbol of a scallop-shell was usually the pilgrim badge for St James of Compostella in Spain. Two pilgrimages to Compostella equalled one to Rome. Two pilgrimages to Rome equalled one to Jerusalem in the Medieval Pilgrimage League Table! The symbol represents the pilgrim on his journey from Earth to Heaven.

SHIP

A ship can symbolise the Christian Church carrying the faithful through the world. It is also symbolic of the ship of life crossing the sea of death and conveying Christ's people safely to the heavenly harbour.

SKELETON

A skeleton represents the inevitability of death. It is a form of symbolism intended to remind us that nothing in this temporal world is of any real value. Only the eternal verities have any real worth.

SKULL

This is also a symbol of impending mortality. Celts believed that the soul resided in the head – Brân the Blessed's severed head was kept on a charger. So was the head of John the Baptist. Vikings made cups from the skulls of their enemies. Like the entire skeleton, the skull reminds us that life is short and that eternal values such as love, truth, and mercy are the only ones that really matter.

SNAKE

The snake is the symbol of health and healing, although it may also remind the faithful of the Serpent in the Garden of Eden, and warn them to be on their guard against temptation.

SUNDIAL

A sundial symbolises the relentless passage of time. Like the skeleton and the skull, it reminds us that time is passing all too quickly, and that death waits for us all.

SWORD

The sword is the symbol of justice and honesty. It represents the act of cutting through hypocrisy and deceit to defend the truth. It reminds the faithful of the need to be honest and straightforward in all they say and do.

TORCH

The Bible reminds us: 'Thy word is a light unto my feet.' and 'A light to lighten the darkness'

TREE

This can relate to the cross of Christ, but it also signifies the Tree of Life in the Garden of Eden.

URN

The symbol of the urn represents a safe repository for the ashes of the dead, preserving them for God until the Day of Resurrection. The urn also symbolises the jar of precious spikenard ointment with which Mary Magdalene anointed the feet of Christ. It therefore symbolises generous giving.

WHEAT

This symbolises bread, the staff of life. It also represents the word of God in Christ's Parable of the Sower. Christ himself is the Bread of Life as symbolised in the Mass. The Priest gives the people this bread with the words: 'The Body of Christ, keep you in eternal life.'

WILLOW

This symbolises grief and mourning. Traditionally, the willow weeps.

WINGS

Wings depict spiritual beings on a divine mission; traditionally Angels were winged beings doing God's work, including carrying the souls of the faithful to Heaven.

WREATH

Because of its circular form, the wreath – like the symbol of the circle – represents eternal life. It has links with the idea of winning an eternal crown of glory in Heaven, rather than a fading crown of earthly success.

Chapter Three

Grave Stories from Mid-Wales

THE CAR PARK HERO – ABERYSTWYTH

James Williams was a young merchantseaman in the mid-nineteenth century, the great days of sail. It is sad and ironic to think that such an adventurous boy eventually landed in a car park. The Church of St Michael and All Angels, Aberystwyth, was once surrounded by a tasteful and dignified graveyard. It is now a repository for commuters' Metros and Mondeos. During the modernisation process – carried out mainly to facilitate the lawnmowers which work on the graves – James's stone was moved from the centre to the south-west corner, and set at an angle in the car-park wall. It doesn't make it exactly easy to find, but when you do locate it, this is what we read:

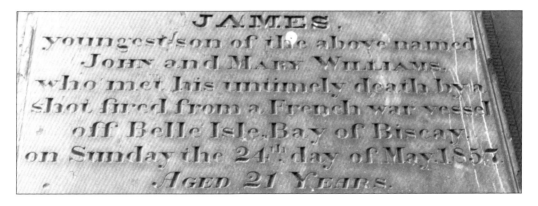

JAMES,
youngest son of the above named
JOHN and MARY WILLIAMS,
who met his untimely death by a
shot fired from a French war vessel
off Belle Isle, Bay of Biscay,
on Sunday the 24th day of May 1857.
AGED 21 YEARS.

This young merchant seaman became the focal point of an international incident. Uncharacteristically, England and France were not at war at the time, but there was a rigorous, continental economic blockade. The French navy were insisting that all vessels approaching Belle Isle, or the French mainland, must identify themselves by flying their national colours.

Julian Williams (great-great-great-nephew of James Williams), a former art director and set-designer with the BBC, explained that as James's ship approached Belle Isle, a French man-of-war was stationed at the entrance to the harbour. In accordance with the conditions of the blockade, the French demanded that James's ship should fly its flag. It failed to do so quickly enough, and the French belligerently fired what was intended to be a warning shot. Tragically, it came far too close, and struck James as he was in the very act of

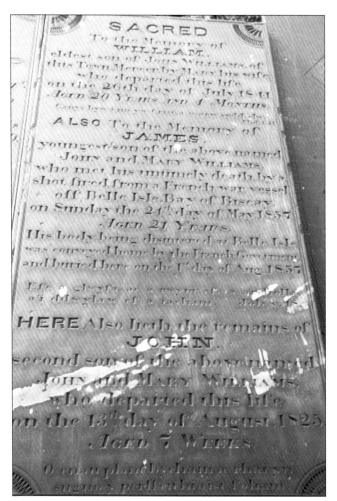

SACRED To the Memory of WILLIAM...

The Williams family graves were marked by this stone, now in the corner of an Aberystwyth car park.

climbing the rigging to unfurl and display the Union Jack. The flag was a vitally important icon to British seamen in those days, and it was actually entwined around James when the fatal French shot went through it.

James's body was originally interred in Belle Isle, but his untimely and unnecessary death caused ructions in Wales and London. The local Cardigan MP remained curiously silent, but Lewis Llewellyn Dillwyn, the Liberal MP for Swansea, brought the matter up in the House of Commons. His concern over young James, and the affront to the British Merchant Navy, stirred up very strong feelings. In consequence, the French Captain responsible had to face a court martial and James's body was returned to Wales by an embarrassed French navy. Their man-of-war sailed slowly and solemnly into Cardigan Bay and anchored off shore on August 1st, 1857, witnessed by thousands of hushed spectators.

James's body was brought ashore by tender and taken up to St Michael's graveyard. The stone which once covered him among a group of Williams family graves in the centre of the cemetery is now laid at an angle as part of the south-west corner of the graveyard. It is a curious quirk of fate that the memorial to this brave young sailor – whom chance had raised to the status of a national hero – should finish up in the car-park wall surrounding his final anchorage.

THE CLASSLESS BROTHERS – LLANIDLOES

Llanidloes, a busy market town in Powys, has been an important junction and meeting-place for many years. It was once the home of the wealthy and influential Onslow family. Their business interests centred on lead mining, and the flamboyant Mrs Onslow was also an heiress in her own right. They literally and metaphorically enjoyed a Rolls-Royce lifestyle. But Death is a great leveller. This is the tragic inscription on the grave of the two young Onslow brothers:

 They were lovely and pleasant in their lives and in their death they were not divided.

This inscription paraphrases King David's lament over Saul and his son, Jonathan, after their deaths in battle, as recorded in the Second Book of Samuel.

The Onslow brothers, Dennis and Ralph Denzil, were killed on 26th January, 1921, in a notorious railway crash at Abermule. The boys were on their way back to Harrow School for the start of the winter term, following their Christmas break at the family seat, Mount Severn. They were on board a train heading south from Shrewsbury. A second train was approaching Abermule from the direction of Aberystwyth. There was a single-track line with a bypass loop at this point, which was intended to allow just one of the trains to have a straight run, while the other was diverted and waited in the loop. On the fateful day, the driver of the Aberystwyth train was wrongly informed that the Shrewsbury train had been delayed and that he had the all-clear to proceed. The railway safety system of token exchange had been disregarded, and human error put the trains on a fatal collision course towards each other. Seventeen people were killed in that horrendous crash – including sixteen-year-old Dennis and seventeen-year-old Ralph Denzil, the Onslow brothers.

They were buried near their home in Llanidloes cemetery, where in those days, a person's final resting-place was determined by his, or her, station in life. First Class Church and First Class Non-conformists were nearest the gate, and then in descending order, socially and geographically, came the Second and Third Class. Mrs Onslow, despite her enormous wealth, found such division upsetting, and was determined to defy this funereal convention. She laid her beloved sons to rest in what was then considered to be the Third Class area of the cemetery. Their mother also defied the convention of wearing black mourning-clothes. She arrived at the graveside in her yellow Rolls-Royce, wearing bright, diaphanous golds and yellows – because those were the colours by which her sons had always known her.

Despite the devastating tragedy, one Onslow child did survive. Influenza had prevented the third Onslow boy from catching the same fatal train as his two brothers.

THEY WERE LOVELY AND PLEASANT IN THEIR LIVES AND IN THEIR DEATH THEY WERE NOT DIVIDED

The memorial stone of the Onslow brothers, Dennis and Ralph Denzil, in Llanidloes cemetery.

Their Names Live On

LAURA ASHLEY – CARNO

The dress designer, interior decorator and businesswoman Laura Ashley was born in 1925 at Dowlais near Merthyr Tydfil as Laura Mountney. She married Bernard Ashley in 1949. Having begun a textile-based company in London, Laura persuaded her husband to move to Wales. They fell in love with the scenery in Powys and re-located to Machynlleth in 1963. Soon after that they settled in Carno. Their first rather modest address was the old railway station but with the phenomenal success of their country-flower and Victorian-print styles, the company eventually grew into a flourishing international concern.

In 1985, Laura Ashley died after a tragic fall at her daughter's Cotswold home. She is buried in the churchyard of St John the Baptist at Carno, a short distance from the factory that bears her name.

THE CIPHERS IN THE STONE – LLANFYLLIN

The red-brick Church of Llanfyllin stands in the main street and is approached from the side via a short flight of steps that is paved with the gravestones of past parishioners. In the early nineteenth century, there was a Victorian fashion for what were then known as *conceits,* compiled from strange alphabets and unfamiliar symbols. The dictionary defines them as 'elaborate metaphors, artistic effects or even fanciful notions.' One of the stones now serving as a step carries this curious inscription:

Genealogist David Petley-Jones took a particular interest in this well-trodden and weathered stone with its puzzling conceit. He wondered whether the unfamiliar letters might be Greek or Hebrew, but soon discovered that they were not. Tackling the problem from the perspective of a scientific cryptographer, he assumed that the first four mysterious characters made up the word 'also' because that would have been normal on any epitaph containing more than one name. Then he assumed that the language concealed by the conceit was English because the rest of the inscription was in English. Now he had tentatively identified the symbols which represented A, L, S and O. He then noted carefully which letters occurred more than once. His knowledge of letter-frequency in normal English usage gave him a major clue: E occurs much more often than any other letter. One of the strange symbols was repeated eight times, which led him to believe that it was an E. This, combined with the A, L, S and O clues, enabled him to tackle the first word after *Margaret*. The probable position of the A and E in this word led him to suspect that it was a clue as to the relationship of Margaret to Catherine and David Edwards: was she their *daughter*? This provided further clues to the decipherment of the symbols for D, U, G, H, T and R. Armed with all these letters, David was able to make an educated guess at the remainder of the conceit.

His next investigation took him to the Parish Registers, and this involved some inspired genealogical mathematics. He knew that Margaret's mother, Catherine Edwards, had died aged 59 in 1856. She must, therefore, have been sixteen in 1813, the earliest year in which she was likely to have married and started a family. Combing the Parish Registers for the appropriate dates, he found that Catherine and David Edwards were recorded as the parents of Margaret. The Registers gave David the birth and death dates for Margaret, and her age when she left this world. Born in 1828, she died in 1834, aged six.

Based on David's decoding, the epitaph says:

 Also Margaret, daughter of the above named, died September 1834, aged 6 yrs.

That's a simple enough epitaph, but it conceals a far from simple story. What also makes this stone and its conceit particularly interesting is that it is clearly an elaborate and expensive piece of work. Yet the Registers show that the child's father, David, was a labourer, living in a small terraced house in Lower Street, Llanfyllin: a very modest home. So how did he afford such a monument? In addition, he was unlikely to have had the advantage of a good education. So how did he work out that intricate coded message on the stone?

David Petley-Jones worked with great skill and determination, applying his expert knowledge and experience in the field to break the code successfully from scratch – no mean feat. As far as he was concerned, the curious letters of the inscription were probably the unique design of David Edwards himself, or some craftsman friend of his . . .

But they weren't!

These strange letters are actually part of a little-known, esoteric alphabet, variously known as the Ancient Theban or Honorian Script, frequently associated with witchcraft, paganism and magic, which raises shadowy question-marks over the fate of young Margaret and her family.

CASTING THE FIRST STONE – PRESTEIGNE

To the memory of Mary Morgan,
who young and beautiful, endowed with a
good understanding and disposition, but
unenlightened by the sacred truths of
Christianity become the victim of sin and
shame and was condemned, to an
ignominious death on the 13th April 1805,
for the murder of her bastard child.

Mary's epitaph is about as judgmental as nineteenth-century humbug and hypocrisy could have devised. The gravestone carrying that condescending inscription stands in St Andrew's churchyard, Presteigne, about 100 metres from the River Lugg, the border of Wales.

Sixteen-year-old Mary worked as an under-cook at Maeslwch Castle, the seat of Walter Wilkins, the MP for Radnorshire. In the early afternoon of Sunday, 23rd September, 1804, Mary was in the kitchen, cleaning and gutting chickens with a small knife. Saying that she felt unwell, she was excused and went up to her bedroom, where she locked the door. A few moments later, she gave birth to a baby girl, but almost immediately afterwards the infant was killed by having her head practically severed from her body. The crime was soon discovered by Mary's horrified workmates.

The local Coroner, who was also the Landlord of the Radnorshire Arms in Presteigne, found Mary responsible for the little girl's death, and she was imprisoned for seven long, arduous months before being sent for trial.

The present Post Office stands on the site of the Old Shire Hall, where the case was heard. It was Mary's first misfortune to come up before the severe and merciless Judge Hardinge, who was alleged by some historians to have had an odd prejudice against women. It was her second misfortune not to conform to the fashionable piety and ostentatious church-going of the time, and her apparent lack of religion and contrition may also have antagonised the Judge.

Mary was one of the many vulnerable young servant girls of her time, who were all too often sexually abused and exploited by their masters. Walter Wilkins junior, the son of her employer, was known to have been attracted to her, but was one of those who served on the jury which found her guilty. The Wilkins family were prominent members of the establishment, and it has been suggested by some researchers that they were involved in a cover-up.

Contradictory evidence, however, exists in the form of a letter written by Judge Hardinge to the Bishop of St Asaph immediately following Mary's execution. In it, the Judge maintains that Mary denied that young Wilkins was the father of her child. According to Hardinge, she had named a fellow-servant, and he had accepted paternity. It also appeared from this letter that far from conspiring with the Wilkins family to cover the matter up, the Judge was critical of what he described as their 'profligate' behaviour.

Whatever deep and dark intrigues may, or may not, have surrounded Mary's case, on April 11th, 1805, she was found guilty. Judge Hardinge not only sentenced her to death, but ordered that after her execution, her body should be sent to the anatomists for dissection. She was duly hanged at noon on Saturday, April 13th, 1805, at Gallows Lane, just west of Presteigne. Among the poignant evidence that still remains are details of the costs involved in her imprisonment and death: her food for 102 of the days of her imprisonment came to £1-5-6 or £1.27 in modern money; and the cost of her shroud, burial cap and coffin bearers was £1-19-0, or £1.95.

It was unusual, even then, for the death sentence actually to be carried out in cases of infanticide. Normally, a Judge would pronounce the death sentence and then grant a reprieve straight afterwards. Hardinge himself had been known to do this in other similar cases.

The long, sanctimonious epitaph on Mary's stone was the work of a friend of the Judge, the Earl of Aylesbury. Was it intended to counter the tide of local protest, and the sense of injustice arising from Mary's execution? But the stone in St Andrew's graveyard is not the real one: it is merely a facsimile. The original one had begun to deteriorate, and was accordingly removed and preserved in what is now the Judge's Lodging – the Town Museum – which was once the dark and dismal jail where she was held.

Just a body's length away from the replica stone stands a smaller stone bearing the inscription:

 He that is without sin among you, let him first cast a stone at her.

It recalls Christ's gentle mercy on the woman accused of adultery, whom the scribes and Pharisees had wanted to stone to death.

That small stone was erected a few years later, perhaps by the townspeople, Mary's parents, or even her defence counsel, Richard Beavan.

St Andrew's churchyard also contains what was intended to be an amusing, or witty, epitaph on the gravestone of William Wilson Johnson, who was buried in 1823, aged seventeen years. It can be found about 20 metres from the gate at the Broad Street entrance.

> My death so suddenly and quick,
> Occasion'd by a horse's kick;
> My Parents dear do not Repent
> My soul so quick to heaven was sent.

Their Names Live On

ROBERT OWEN – NEWTOWN

Born in 1771, Robert Owen grew up to become a magnificently generous and caring man, a visionary who wanted to reform the world. Best described as a socialist, an industrialist and a philanthropist, Owen eventually went home to die in 1858 in his beloved Newtown after a long life spent on behalf of those in need. He lies beside his parents, in the old churchyard of St Mary's, which had to be abandoned in 1840 because of the floods. The Owen graves are not far from the River Severn, and Robert's deservedly became a place of pilgrimage. The Co-op erected impressive artistic railings around it in 1902. There is another very fitting memorial to him in Kensal Green cemetery in London. It reads:

> He organised infants schools. He secured the reduction of the hours of labour for women and children in factories. He was a liberal supporter of the earliest efforts to obtain national education. He laboured to promote international arbitration. He was one of the foremost Britons who taught men to aspire to a higher social state by reconciling the interests of capital and labour. He spent his life and a large fortune in seeking to improve his fellowmen by giving them education, self-reliance, and moral worth. His life was sanctified by human affection and lofty effort.

Chapter Four

Grave Stories from South-east Wales

OUTWITTING THE DEVIL – MONMOUTH

Historic Monmouth is an important market town in Gwent, and the famous Monnow Bridge is its gateway. The town itself is dominated by the impressive spire of St Mary's Church, and in the shadow of that spire lies one of the most elaborate and complex grave inscriptions anywhere in Wales.

 Here lies John Renie.

That basic statement seems simple and straightforward enough – but not when its letters are engraved over and over again inside a rectangular frame consisting of nineteen columns and fifteen rows: making 285 letters altogether. Taking the letters of *Here lies John Renie* and laying them out as a permutation makes it possible to reach a vast number of different arrangements. If we think of a simple group of letters such as A,B and C, they can be written as ABC, ACB, BAC, BCA, CAB and CBA. As more letters are added, the number of possible permutations goes up astronomically. The five letters in the name RENIE, for example, can be arranged in 120 different ways. The 285 letters on the stone have been calculated to be capable of producing well over 40,000 combinations. Like word puzzles in modern magazines, John's inscription can be read vertically, horizontally, diagonally and in little pathways that run back on themselves and cross over themselves. So John Renie seems to have been a complex character.

The curious coded stone of John Renie which can be read in thousands of ways

John was a glazier, and a decorative and house painter, who lived and worked in Monnow Street, the main trading thoroughfare of the town. He had a wife and four children. Renie lived during a time of active political and social reform, and was involved with the early Friendly Society movement. In the days before Trades Unions and the Welfare State, people banded together to form mutual aid-groups to help and support one another at times of injury, sickness or bereavement. The Independent Odd Fellows, branch number 106, was John's Monmouth group, and he served them as a part-time actuary. This work involved calculating the risks associated with various ages, trades and professions, and the necessary mathematics were often displayed on actuarial tables. This may be a clue to John's ability to design such an elaborate and complicated epitaph; a similar one-off stone today would cost thousands of pounds.

In addition to his professional skills, John was a dedicated reformer, who worked tirelessly for liberal reform. As his obituary records, it was Renie's unremitting zeal that secured the election of 'B.Hall Esq, the Reform Candidate'. Tragically, the cost was high. Renie succumbed to stress and overwork, and died while still a young man.

His epitaph also records that he died on May **31**, 1**832,** aged **33**: an uncanny sequence which almost suggests that he calculated his own demise.

In addition to his strong social conscience, Renie was a devoutly religious man, and in the early nineteenth-century religion was acutely concerned with death, hell and judgement. There were those who believed that the devil could be outwitted by curious, jumbled, coded inscriptions which would hinder the dark one's identification of the deceased – until he or she had safely escaped into Heaven! Wall burials were once believed to have served the same purpose: a wall was technically *nowhere*, being neither inside nor outside the building.

Finding John on Judgement Day has been rendered even more difficult because his stone no longer stands over his body. Years after John's death, during a reorganisation of St Mary's Churchyard, the stone was moved about 100 metres eastwards from its original position near the west door and now lies that much nearer to Jerusalem.

THE KING OF TERRORS – CEFN GOLAU, TREDEGAR

This is a unique and lonely cemetery, set on bleak moorland beyond and above the town. The bodies that lie here were rejected by the Tredegar chapels and churches because it was believed that they were contaminated with Asiatic Cholera – the nineteenth-century King of Terrors. The epidemic had swept across Europe, reached England and arrived in Wales in the autumn of 1832. Mystery was part of its terror. No-one knew what caused it, how it was spread, or how to stop it.

Tredegar by 1830 had grown from a small village to a critically overcrowded

The lonely cholera cemetery above Tredegar: court of the King of Terrors.

town of over 10,000 inhabitants. Most of them depended for their livelihood upon coal-mining and the local iron works. Living conditions were appalling for those poor workers and their large families. There was no provision for sewerage, no clean piped water, and no provision for Public Health. The disease first took hold among the overcrowded terraced houses in Charles Street. Although those houses were recently demolished, pathetic remnants can still be found where they once stood.

The King of Terrors was characterised by its killing speed. A victim could be walking around in good health in the morning and be dead by nightfall. Because cholera struck without warning, there were some who began to interpret it as an Act of God – and supposed that it was divine retribution for a life of insufficient holiness.

Up at the Cefn Golau cholera cemetery, the remains of the iron railings which once encircled it can still be traced. Beyond this perimeter, the jagged, broken stones now lie at odd, irregular angles – like a miniature Stonehenge after an earthquake. Several hundred victims lie here, but only a few score of their stones are visible today. One of the clearest and most legible epitaphs tells the tragic story of Thomas James, a twenty-year-old roll-turner at the iron works, who died in the epidemic of 1832.

One night and day I bore great pain:
To try for cure was all in vain,
But God knew what to me was best,
Did ease my pain and gave me rest.

To find out more, we made for the Council Offices, where we knew there was an exhibition of photographs depicting the history of Tredegar. The display area was presided over by the impressive bust of Aneurin (Nye) Bevan (1897-1960) architect of the National Health Service – and a famous son of Tredegar. There we found an interesting picture of a Cefn Golau cholera grave. The epitaph gave the name of William Thomas, a wheelwright, who had been the first victim of the epidemic. But strangely, we could not recall seeing the stone shown in the photograph while we had been exploring at Cefn Golau. We went back to the cemetery for another look – dodging the mountain ponies who were in the habit of using the stones as scratching posts, and were responsible for toppling some of them. Once again, we drew a blank. Where was William Thomas?

Following a call from Aaron Jones, a local historian and council employee, we made a rendezvous with him by the famous Tredegar Town Clock, and followed him into the Library Museum. There we found a broken tombstone in three sections. When we pieced it together, this is what it revealed:

William Thomas Wheelwright late of Swansea who departed this life at Tredegar Iron Works, October 21st, 1832, aged 38 years. He was the first to die of the cholera and was interred in this burial ground. This stone was placed at the expense of his friends at the Tredegar Iron Works

Cholera struck Tredegar twice more in the 1840s before medical science discovered that the King of Terrors travelled as a micro-organism via polluted water, damp clothing and the profuse sweat of dying victims.

SERGEANT MAJOR OF STEEL – EBBW VALE

Warrant Officer Class II, Williams, J.H., of the 10th Battalion South Wales Borderers remains the most highly-decorated serviceman in Wales. During a very distinguished service career, he achieved four major awards for gallantry, the most prestigious being the Victoria Cross, which he was awarded near the end of World War One.

John, popularly known as Jack, was born on 29th December, 1886 in Nantyglo in what was then Monmouthshire. His mother, Elizabeth, was a schoolteacher, and Jack was educated at Brierly Hill School, Ebbw Vale. He started work aged twelve in the smithy of Marine Colliery. In 1906 he enlisted in

ANEURIN BEVAN

It was a century after the last major cholera outbreak that pioneering moves towards improving public health led to Nye Bevan's epoch-making success in introducing the National Health Service in 1946. He felt so passionate about a totally free health service that he resigned from the Cabinet in 1951 over the introduction of prescription charges. Despite this resignation he went on to become Deputy Leader of the Labour Party in 1959 – barely a year before his tragic death in Chesham, Buckinghamshire. Nye was cremated near Tredegar and his ashes were scattered above the town in the Duffryn Hills, where he had conducted so many open-air meetings attended by vast crowds of his supporters. Four massive rocks mark the spot. The central monolith carries these words:

> IT WAS HERE
>
> ANEURIN BEVAN
>
> SPOKE TO THE PEOPLE
>
> OF HIS CONSTITUENCY AND THE WORLD

His wife, Jennie Lee, who went on to become Minister for the Arts in Harold Wilson's Labour Government, was also responsible for establishing the Open University. She died in 1988, aged 84. Jennie was also cremated and her ashes were scattered in the same area as Aneurin's.

Nye Bevan has a family connection with the cholera graves at Cefn Golau: his grandfather erected the iron railings which once guarded those bleak and lonely graves.

the South Wales Borderers, but, after a short spell of duty, bought his discharge. From there, he went to Cwm Colliery to work as their blacksmith. When hostilities began, Jack rejoined his old regiment in November 1914. A year later he was promoted to Sergeant, and in 1917 he became Company Sergeant Major. During this time, he took part in the renowned attack on Mametz Wood and the Battle for Paschendael, for which he was decorated.

The action which won him his Victoria Cross took place on October 8th, 1918. At Villers Outreaux, his platoon was pinned down in uncut barbed wire and under heavy German machine-gun fire. They were sustaining heavy casualties, and Jack ordered a Lewis gun to engage the enemy, while he himself charged the German post single-handedly. He took them on the flank and captured fifteen men. His prisoners suddenly realised that he was on his own, and attacked him. They soon discovered that it was not a good idea to take on a Welsh colliery blacksmith. Jack bayoneted five of his assailants, and the ten survivors promptly surrendered again. Soon afterwards, the South Wales Borderers and the rest of the Brigade swept triumphantly into the village. Jack was awarded the Victoria Cross for his action. The inscription on the medal simply reads: 'For Valour'.

After the war ended, even returning heroes did not find life easy. Jack worked as a rent collector before being appointed as a Commissionaire in the general office of the Richard Thompson Baldwin Steel Company in Ebbw Vale.

He died in March 1953 in Saint Woolo's Hospital in Newport. The Army which he had served so well gave him a good send-off, but his grave was modest, and his military honours were not recorded on it. However, the local branch of the British Legion in Ebbw Vale took it upon themselves to raise the necessary funds to furnish Jack with an appropriate memorial, which lists his Distinguished Service Medal, Military Medal and Bar and his Victoria Cross.

At the Royal Regiment of Wales (24th/41st Foot) Museum, Brecon, the South Wales Borderers record their history and preserve their trophies – including those from the famous engagement at Rorke's Drift in Africa, where they won seven Victoria Crosses. All of Jack's medals are on display here, but the VC in the case is a replica. The real one is locked away in the Regimental safe.

ROMAN REMAINS – CAERLEON AND BULMORE

In AD 43 the Romans invaded Britain with 40,000 men led by Aulus Plautius. Twenty years later, as the Romans approached Wales, the fiercely heroic Celtic Silurians put up stubborn resistance, but were eventually overcome by the Second Augustan Legion. This Legion had been brought across from its German base at Strasbourg before making its way to Wales. Caerleon soon became one of the largest Roman military installations in Britain, and was occupied for over 200 years. It was an extensive complex built and maintained by the soldiers themselves because, in addition to their fighting troops, the Legions contained skilled craftspeople such as surveyors, architects, water engineers, tile makers, plumbers and carpenters, all assisted by general labourers.

A population in excess of 5,000 eventually constructed barracks, workshops, a hospital and elaborate Roman-style bathing facilities. Shortly after reaching South Wales, the Legion was joined by its camp followers: traders, wives, families and mistresses. This large military base provided opportunities for the

Memorial tablets in the Roman Legionary Museum in Caerleon.

indigenous population to supply the army on a profitable basis. Local men were also able to enrol as military auxiliaries. This gave them a reasonably secure future in a dangerous and unpredictable world.

After a Roman Legionary had completed 25 years of satisfactory service, he was entitled to retire to a Veterans' Settlement. These would always be located close to the fortress for mutual protection. Such a settlement existed just over a mile away from Caerleon at Great Bulmore on the other side of the River Usk. The present population is accommodated in just two family homes, but there was once a large enough community in the area to need its own cemetery. In a Roman workshop which was found opposite the site, it was noted that the floor was paved with large rectangular stones. These were lifted by archaeologists who were surprised to find that the lower sides – previously hidden in the earth – were inscribed. These were the gravestones of the Roman soldiers themselves.

Fashions for the disposal of the dead changed as time passed. For the first two centuries, cremation was practised, and the remains were placed in pots or jars and buried in the ground. Some of these containers were equipped with a leaden pipe, which went all the way up to the surface, where it was embellished with an ornamental funnel, down which libations were poured. As it was believed that the dead could be sustained on their journey to the afterlife by food and drink of the kind which had sustained them on Earth, gifts of milk, honey and wine were poured down these libation pipes.

At the end of the second century, burials took place inside stone coffins, or bodies were placed directly in the ground. In both eventualities, the sites were marked with appropriately inscribed stones. Of the soldiers whose gravestones have been found in the Caerleon area, three died in their twenties, five in their thirties and forties, three were over sixty and one reached the grand old age of 100. Some stones also commemorate wives and families.

Roman epitaphs habitually begin with the letters D. M. standing for *Dis Manibus* which means 'To the spirits of the Departed'. This part of the inscription is intended to sanctify the memorial. This D. M. is then followed by the personal and military details of the deceased. The following stones are on display at Caerleon's Roman Legionary Museum and were described to us by historian, Richard J. Brewer.

Ō. ꟽ. Aurelius Ꟶerculanus
Aeques vixit annos XXVIII coniux
Faciendum curavit

To the Spirits of the departed Aurelius Herculanus, horseman, lived 28 years, his wife had this set up.

Ō.ꟽ. Tadia Vallaunius vixit annos LXV et
Tadius Exuperatus Filius vixit annos XXXVII
defunctus expeditione Germanica Tadia
Exuperata Filia matri et Fratri piissima secus
tumulum patris posuit.

To the spirits of the departed Tadia Vallaunius lived 65 years and Tadius Exuperatus her son lived 37 years having died on the German expedition. Tadia Exuperata the devoted daughter set this up to her mother and brother beside her father's tomb.

The Celts relied on their oral traditions and used no writing. It was the Romans who brought the Latin alphabet to Wales, and so it is to them that we owe our ability to read these inscriptions from nearly 2000 years ago – the oldest epitaphs that we are able to understand.

HANDS DIPPED IN BLOOD – LLANGWM

In the churchyard of St Jerome's is a stone recording the despicable murder of an 84-year-old woman, Elizabeth Gwin of Pwl in 1743. She was killed in her own home, which is now said to be haunted by her troubled spirit. Her epitaph reads:

Here lieth the Body that lost its life
By bloddy Villain full of strife
Who coveted boath gold and land
As anybody may understand.
Wo be to those infernall foes
Who dipt their hands in blood
The King of Kings who knows all things
One day on them will vengeance bring.

A FAVOURITE CHARGER – NEWPORT, GWENT

Tredegar House, one of the finest stately homes in Wales, is the ancestral seat of the Morgan family, who made their money from coal and property. Today, the house is in the care of Newport Council and is well worth a visit to admire the lavish interiors. But at the back of the house, surrounded by a circular hedge of evergreens, are two monuments. The larger one is a white marble obelisk dedicated to Sir Briggs – a horse. The smaller stone was raised to Peeps, the dog. The large obelisk to Sir Briggs shows a bas-relief of a cavalry horse being stroked appreciatively by his rider. The inscription reads:

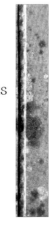

In memory of
Sir Briggs
A favourite charger he carried his master
The Hon. Godfrey Morgan, Captain 17th Lancers
Boldly and well at the Battle of the Alma
In the first line in the light cavalry charge of
Balaclava, and at the Battle of Inkerman 1854.
He died at Tredegar Park February 8th 1874
Aged 28 years

Sir Briggs, the valiant cavalry horse, was in the front line during the famous Charge of the Light Brigade, sensationally popularised by Alfred Lord Tennyson, the then Poet Laureate.

Godfrey Morgan was the second heir in line to the Tredegar family fortune. He served as a Captain in the 17th Lancers, and when hostilities broke out in the Crimean War (1854-6) he sailed for the Ukraine with two horses from the magnificently ornate family stable: Atheist, his number one mount, succumbed on the long, arduous voyage to the Black Sea, and was tossed overboard with other dead horses.

The British and their allies, the French and Turks, were seeking to curtail Russian influence in the Mediterranean region. During the Battle of Balaclava, the 17th Lancers were part of the Light Cavalry Brigade that charged suicidally down the wrong valley towards well-deployed Russian guns. Tactically, they were meant to have attacked a completely different target, but because of a misunderstood order, they galloped fearlessly towards the enemy cannon in their direct line of sight. Inevitably, the guns took the lives of nearly 400 cavalrymen. Miraculously, just over 200 survived the death or glory charge.

This obelisk commemorates Sir Briggs, the brave horse who brought Captain Godfrey Morgan safely back from the Charge of the Light Brigade.

Captain Godfrey, who rode in the front line, wrote to his father after the battle, and told him that although he had come through unscathed, Sir Briggs had sustained a sabre cut to his head, from which, in due course, he made a good recovery.

The survivors of that incomparable charge moved from history into legend as a result of Tennyson's stirring poem:

> . . . Theirs not to reason why,
> Theirs but to do and die.
> Into the Valley of Death
> Rode the six hundred.

Those who had taken part enjoyed celebrity status in Victorian Britain.

The painting in the entrance hall at Tredegar House complements Tennyson's great poem by graphically depicting the heroic charge, like a scene from a Hollywood action film with Captain Godfrey played by Russell Crowe.

Even in old age, Captain Godfrey and his recollections of Sir Briggs were inseparable. One of the most poignant mementoes on display on the wall of Tredegar House is a photograph of the elderly Captain framed by the horseshoe of the gallant steed which brought him safely back from Balaclava. Another impressive link with those momentous days which visitors can see is Sir Briggs's saddlecloth bearing the defiant emblem of the 17th Lancers: a gaunt skull implying the motto 'Death or Glory'.

The small stone beside Sir Briggs's impressive obelisk is inscribed:

In loving memory of Peeps
Fondest and most affectionate of Skye Terriers
Who died September 6th 1898
His honest heart was all his master's own
There are some both good and wise who say
Dumb creatures we have cherished here below
Shall give us joyous greeting when we reach the
Golden Gate.

Captain Godfrey Morgan was rightly respected for his courage and coolness during the Charge of the Light Brigade. Another equally admirable aspect of his character was revealed by his affection for the animals whose companionship enriched his life.

THE SPENT BLACKSMITH – LLANFIHANGEL CRUCORNEY

Just north of Abergavenny on the Hereford road stands the Church of St Michael, only a tankard's throw from the Skirrid Inn, the oldest hostelry in Wales. A gravestone from 1766 is set inside the porch and dedicated to the village blacksmith – a craftsman on whom many would have depended in those days.

My Sledge and Hammer lies Reclin'd
My Bellows too have lost his wind
My Fires extinct, my Forge decay'd
And in ye Dust, my Vice is laid.
My Coal is Spent, my Iron is gone
My Nails Are Drove, my Work is Done.

The words of the epitaph are attributed to the poet William Hayley (1745 – 1820).

TAKING HIS NAP – CWMYOY

On a hillside in the Vale of Ewyas, stands, and that is a generous way of putting it, the church of St Martin. The area was prone to landslip and the church has come off worse than most buildings here. It lurches at impossible angles. One of the early gravestones below the tottering structure dates from 1682 and records:

Thomas Price he takes his nap
In our common mother lap
Awaiting to heare the bridegroom say
Awake my dear and come away.

Their Names Live On

CHARLES STEWART ROLLS – LLANGATTOCK-VIBON-AVEL

The name Rolls-Royce is synonymous with elegance and unsurpassed engineering skill. Charles Stewart Rolls (1877-1910) was the third son of Baron Llangattock who lived at The Hendre, not far from Monmouth. Charles was one of the most significant automobile pioneers in Britain. He set up his own car-building business first and then went on to become the co-founder of Rolls-Royce Limited at the age of 27 in 1904. His brilliantly successful and talented young life ended at Bournemouth in a tragic flying accident when he was only 33, and history records him as the first British aviator to die in this way. His body lies beside St Cadoc's Church in the village of Llangattock-Vibon-Avel among other members of the Llangattock Family, marked by an imposing cluster of stately Celtic crosses. His inscription reads:

In memory of
Charles Stewart Rolls
Third Son of 1st Baron Llangattock
Born August 27 1877. Died July 12 1910.
Blessed are the pure in heart
For they shall see God

Perhaps the superb cars and aero-engines which proudly bear his name are his most enduring memorial.

Chapter Five

Grave Stories from West Wales

ALAS, POOR HESLOP – LLANDYFRIOG

The tomb of Thomas Heslop, killed unfairly in the last duel in Wales.

There was a tendency in the early nineteenth century to write epitaphs based on re-workings of Shakespearean quotations. This was far from new, even then. A century earlier, Nahum Tate (Poet Laureate from 1692 until 1715) had already re-written *King Lear* so extensively that his version had a happy ending. The lines on Thomas Heslop's stone are drawn from *Hamlet*. The anguished Danish Prince is talking to a grimly pragmatic grave-digger when they find a skull which the sexton identifies as Yorick, the King's jester. Hamlet delivers the famous lines:

> Alas, poor Yorick. I knew him, Horatio, a fellow of infinite jest, of most excellent fancy. He hath bore me on his back a thousand times, and now – how abhorred in my imagination it is. My gorge rises at it. Here hung those lips that I have kissed I know not how oft. Where be your gibes now . . . ?

SARAH JANE REES (CRANOGWEN) – LLANGRANOG

An urn surmounts the solemn black stone which commemorates a remarkable, sea-faring woman who lies buried in St Cranog's churchyard. Golden letters pick out these words:

> Safai ar ei phen ei hun ymhlith
> merched a gwragedd y genedl mewn
> athrylith a dawn. Meddai cymeriad
> diystaen a bu yn darlithio, pregethu
> ac ysgrifennu am dros 50 mlynedd

> She stood on her own amongst the
> women and wives of the nation in
> genius and talent. Her character
> was without blemish and she
> lectured, preached and wrote for
> over 50 years.

Sarah Jane Rees (1839 – 1916) was born and raised on a smallholding only a mile from the sea which was destined to feature so prominently in her determined and talented life. Her father owned a small ketch, which enabled him to trade profitably along the Welsh coast. The family prospered and moved to a fine house. Her parents wanted Sarah to be a dressmaker, but she had other ideas, which included higher education. Her studies took her to Ladies' Colleges in Chester and Liverpool, then to a Nautical School in London. There she qualified as a sea captain, and was awarded a Master's Certificate. The sea was in her blood, and she had a pronounced gift for navigation. Over and above her love of maritime adventures, she had a great concern for people – especially the under-privileged. She came home to teach at Pontgarreg School, and, despite the chauvinism of the School Committee, became a Headmistress.

Over and above her regular educational work at the school, Sarah improvised by using local barns, village halls, and any other buildings she could find as make-shift teaching rooms. This flexibility enabled her to teach young farm boys and rural labourers basic literacy, numeracy, and maritime science. She even taught advanced navigation to sea captains who came to her primary school after the children had gone home. Her knowledge extended far beyond mere theory. She sailed with her father, and, on occasion, over-ruled his seamanship when she knew that he was wrong. She commanded respect in this sea-faring community.

Her father was fond of the bottle, and this prompted her to join the Temperance Movement. She would take a pony and trap from the Pentre Arms in Llangranog and travel as far as Tregaron to preach her message. Her concern was not so much with trying to prevent people from having a social drink, as with the excessive consumption of alcohol which she associated with the suffering of battered wives and abused, neglected children.

In 1879 she founded a woman's magazine, *Y Frythones*. It nurtured women's writing talents, and enabled them through their articles and stories to participate in public life, and explore issues outside the home. Her editorial work and interest in literature spilled over into other parts of her life. In keeping with the Eisteddfodic tradition of the *nom de plume*, Sarah was known as *Cranogwen*, an affectionate tribute linking her to her native village.

As she grew older, Sarah became more adventurous and travelled across the Atlantic to lecture and preach in the USA. The money she made on these tours was ploughed back into her village community. Chapels, vestries and even bridges were constructed or repaired as a result of her generous gifts, the greatest of which was the knowledge she passed on to her many students. So effective was her encouragement and maritime teaching that it was said, with some truth, that there was not a sea, or ocean, anywhere in the world where Cranogwen's captains had not sailed.

Thomas Heslop was the last man in Wales to die in a duel. We know from the Burial Register that he was West Indian, but there is no record of whether he was of African or European descent. What we do know, however, is that he was invited over from his home in Carmarthen for a day's partridge-shooting with John Beynon and some Cardiganshire friends. During the course of the day, some of the sportsmen had better opportunities than others, and Thomas Heslop felt disgruntled. After their day's sport, the party adjourned to the Old Salutation Inn at Newcastle Emlyn. The atmosphere soon deteriorated: Heslop maintained that the Cardis had been given better opportunities to shoot game than he had. Beynon mistakenly attempted to defuse the situation by teasing the barmaid as a diversion. Heslop took exception to this, and the men started trading serious insults. Things reached a climax when Heslop challenged Beynon to a duel. A place and date were appointed beside the River Teifi, and seconds were named.

The two men met on opposite sides of a small stream. Pistols were handed out, and each was instructed to face his opponent, turn away from him, walk ten paces, turn again and fire. Beynon took only *five* paces before he turned and shot Heslop in the back. The wound proved fatal.

Word of Beynon's trickery soon got out – possibly spread by Heslop's seconds – and there was a local outcry, which resulted in a court case. The Judge's notes record that Prisoner John Beynon was charged with manslaughter by 'shooting Thomas Heslop with a leaden bullet discharged from a pistol'. His associates, John Walters and James Hughes, were accused of 'abetting and assisting John Beynon in so shooting'.

Local historian, Ken Jones, who helped us to unravel this story, explained that because Beynon was well-connected and knew the local magistrates, he seemed to have got away with it. The outraged locals thought otherwise and after running the gauntlet, Beynon went into hiding and eventually fled to America.

Thomas Heslop's chest tomb stands prominently in the churchyard of St Tyfriog bearing its pathetic, and now barely visible message: *Alas, poor Heslop.*

In 1844, thirty years after Heslop's untimely death, duelling was made illegal in Wales.

STARBUCKS – MILFORD HAVEN

Most of us today are familiar with Starbucks coffee shops, but the name also features notably in Melville's *Moby Dick*. This graphic story of whaling and vengeance includes a notable character among the courageous but misguided seamen: First Mate Starbuck was a devout Quaker. The shape of Milford Haven is largely due to members of that dedicated and hard-working religious movement, generations of whom lie in the Quaker graveyard above the town.

The Society of Friends' cemetery in Milford Haven.

In 1792, Charles Greville, the local land-agent, had plans to develop the port and increase trade with America and Ireland. He persuaded a 100 Quaker seamen and their families to sail from Nantucket Island on the American Eastern Seaboard and settle in Milford Haven. The Quakers, as pacifists, had felt persecuted at home because their refusal to fight for American independence had been regarded by their fellow colonists as disloyalty.

Their main occupation was whaling, and they searched the southern oceans for sperm whales. The blubber was turned into oil and stored in barrels on board, while they sailed back to Milford Haven. From there, it was shipped off to London merchants and often sold on for street lighting. In addition to the commercial value of the oil, whalebone was sold profitably to the makers of fashionable corsets.

Among the Quakers of Milford Haven, the Starbucks were a leading family, who contributed substantially to the reconstruction of the town with its grid-system street plan. Their other interests extended to businesses as diverse as banking, dock-building, brick-making and baking. As the Quaker community became more and more firmly established, they built a Friends' Meeting House for regular worship and fellowship.

The Society of Friends (the Quakers' official title) has no clergy and no set form of service, but their worship typically begins with silence followed by a reading from a book on Quaker faith and practice. The simplicity of their faith was reflected in the simple inscriptions on their earliest graves, such as:

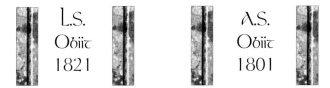

Here is a slightly later one from the burial garden behind their Meeting House, showing how the original basic information had been expanded:

Ironically, these pacifists came to Wales and prospered while Britain was at war with France. By 1815, the war was over. London merchants found alternative sources of oil and the Quakers of Milford Haven suffered financially as a result of this market change. Though some remained in the town, others slipped quietly back to the now politically stable and tolerant American East Coast.

LIFE'S BITTER CUP – NEVERN

The Reverend David Griffith was Vicar of St Brynach's Church in Nevern, famous for its 'bleeding' yew tree, and ornate Celtic Cross dedicated to an eleventh-century notable, but a far more poignant memorial is to be found among the tombs of the Griffith and Bowen

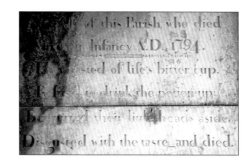

families. Poetry is often used to express emotions beyond the reach of ordinary prose, and one of the Griffith epitaphs records the tragically early deaths of two of the Reverend Griffith's children:

They tasted of life's bitter cup
Refused to drink the potion up
But turned their little heads aside
Disgusted with the taste and died.

The famous Celtic Cross at Nevern.

David, their father, wrote that epitaph for his son and daughter, Anna Letitia and George who died in infancy during the 1780s. Their mother, the heiress Anne Bowen, a frail, delicate woman, was devastated by the loss and never fully recovered, although she later had other children. Infant mortality was a grim fact of life before the medical advances of the twentieth century. Children regularly succumbed to cholera, smallpox, typhoid, respiratory infections, dysentery and other fatal diseases. Without antibiotics or intravenous treatments to re-hydrate patients, children died as a matter of course, and society resignedly accepted the fact. Remedies were largely ineffective. Diseases just took their course and only the lucky ones survived.

Books of condolence intended to comfort parents who had lost their children sold in greater numbers at that time than books of advice on childcare do today. Religious and moral guidance in those times also urged children 'to be kind to their little brothers and sisters because they would not be here for very long'.

(For details of graves demonstrating the extent of child mortality see Chapter Seven on North Wales.)

The fact that such tragedies were widespread and all too frequent does not mask the force with which they struck each bereaved individual. Anne Griffith died while still suffering from the depression which had blighted her life since her children's death. A few years later, David moved into a fine house named Berry Hill, with his wife's sisters, Elizabeth and Jane. Even the good company and comfortable lifestyle of his new home failed to lift his spirits. He wrote: 'I feel laid aside as worthless.' Eventually, being unable to derive any satisfaction from life, he hanged himself at Berry Hill on the 18th September, 1834, and was buried in Nevern churchyard mourned by a crowd of 3000 people.

Ironically, one of David and Anne's *surviving* children, another George, who had risen to become a JP of the County of Pembrokeshire, concluded his epitaph on the wall of St Brynach's Church with the admonition to 'watch and pray because time is short.' By the standards of the day, his time wasn't: he lived to be 67.

Their Names Live On

DYLAN THOMAS – LAUGHARNE

One of the best known poets ever, Dylan Thomas was born in 1914 in Cwmdonkin Drive, Swansea. Towards the end of his life, in 1949, he settled at Laugharne, where he lived in The Boathouse and wrote in his garden shed overlooking the estuary of the River Taf. He died in New York in 1953, but was brought home and buried in the churchyard of St Martin's in Laugharne, where his grave is marked by a plain white wooden cross. For a man who was capable of writing immortal lines like 'And death shall have no dominion' and 'Do not go gentle into that good night', his epitaph is minimalist, albeit in Gothic script.

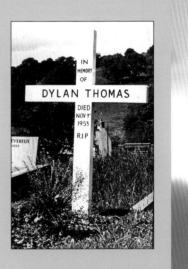

Chapter Six

Masons, Monuments and Materials

Of all materials, stone is the most natural and durable. It is part of the Earth that surrounds us. We use it for our homes and our places of work and it covers many of us when we reach our final resting-place.

Stone of some sort is available in almost every part of the country and gravestones have usually been made from locally-quarried material.

Some stones are suitable for carving but they weather badly, especially sandstones. Limestone is soft when quarried and hardens with exposure but is not as long-lasting as the stone of choice in Wales. Slate makes ideal gravestones because it is durable, it weathers well and it is easy to work.

Gwynedd has some great examples that feature beautiful lettering and superb embellishment on headstones in church and chapel yards. Those around Bethesda are particularly fine. Some of these monuments are close on two hundred years old but look as fresh today as they did when they were first cut. In contrast, the soft stones of the Welsh Marches around Presteigne and district are flaking, cracking and being worn down by the elements and time. This is especially true on those stones facing south and west. Future generations will not be able to see or read what we can today.

The work of monumental masons from the late 1600s was a craft development of the church and cathedral carving of the eleventh and twelfth centuries and some of those styles can be traced back to our pagan roots. Carved heads and foliage have been the stock in trade of stone sculptors ever since the

Robert Williams's gravestone at Llandegai. An example of the stone mason's durable art. (See page 62)

47

material was first worked. Winged cherubs and biblical symbols expanded the vocabulary. Throughout Wales, both primitive and sophisticated designs and their interpretation await the discerning eye.

Country churchyards have a natural beauty about them. They are organic places that look as though they grew out of the very ground that they stand in. The stone of the graves blends with the walls and the ancient buildings in a harmony of colour and texture. They tell you where you are. The old red sandstone in east Gwent is one of the most distinctive rocks but limestone and slate have their obvious regional qualities too.

With the development of railways and canals, new materials became available from 1780 onwards. Granite, Dorset and York stones and Marble have all infiltrated Welsh cemeteries. Now there are rows of memorials made from foreign slabs which have upset the continuity of the traditional landscape in our rural places of rest. These newer stones often have highly polished surfaces which do not allow nature to get a grip and soften the surface or give it a colour that fits in with the surroundings.

Granites, now so widespread, come in blues, greys or blacks and are available in various finishes. It was once considered a material that was too hard to work but with diamond-edged saws and power tools this has become the standard stone in most masons' catalogues. Northern England and Scotland used to provide us with this ubiquitous stone for use on graves. Today pre-cut stones shaped as hearts, crosses, ovals and standard rectangles are imported from China and India. These granites are available in hot colours too. Reds, oranges and various speckled finishes are being worked on around the country. We were told by a well-established monumental masonry company that it is quicker and cheaper to import these stones from the Far East than it is to acquire slate from North Wales.

The materials used in memorials have changed over the years and fashion in lettering has constantly altered too. Since the first rough-cut inscriptions of the late sixteenth century the spread of new styles and ideas seems to have gone hand in hand with developments in printing. Early work has a crude charm and the arrangement of the words varies. Letters are inscribed in characters that seem to run out of space on some stones. Word endings can be found in margins or above an incoming word or even contracted in spelling.

The flowery, copper-plate handwriting – so popular in the eighteenth century – seems to have influenced the craft of the mason. The inscriptions from this period are usually elegant in design and have a biting clarity on the best examples. The Classical revival that reached its height in Georgian Britain in stately homes was seen in chapels and churches too. Urns, columns and drapes gave rise to pattern books for both sculptures and lettering. Printed catalogues replaced handwritten manuals, and showed masons how curls and squiggles might enhance a basic script and turn it into a minor art-form.

Graves come in all shapes and sizes. Headstones are usually rectangular or square and are vertical when installed. The most effective of them can be traced back to the ancient artistic concept known as the golden section, which is also called the golden ratio, the golden mean and the divine proportion. Stones with this ratio are especially pleasing to look at because of the perfect mathematical relationship of their dimensions. Having considered the theoretical ideal, there is just as much visual appeal in a picturesque old slab which has been cracked and tilted over the centuries.

Robber's grave at St Nicholas's Church, Montgomery.

One of the oldest epitaphs dedicated to a Celt stands on a hill overlooking the church of Penbryn, near Llangranog. In the middle of a field, opposite a caravan park stands a lone upright stone with a slightly rounded top. The epitaph is written in Latin down the length of the headstone, and the translation tells us that:

 The body of Corbalengus lies here - An Ordovician.

The Ordovicians were the local Celtic tribe and the Latin script suggests the beginning of a Christian tradition in the area. When the site was excavated, cremated remains were found which have been dated to AD 150.

Ledgers are horizontal slabs that are level with the ground. In Victorian times, they were an effective deterrent against body-snatchers or Resurrectionists as they were melodramatically known. Being too heavy to lift, they would have been passed over, literally, in favour of other graves. Railings were also put around graves for the same reason.

To deal with the problem of invasive vegetation some ledgers were raised above ground just a few inches. Some were raised even higher in a mirror of the design of altar tombs inside churches. These are known as chest or table tombs. The bodies still lie six feet under ground and not, as some people think, inside the wall of the tomb which is hollow. On the Welsh borders and reaching over into England, there are bale tombs. These are ornately carved and have semi-circular capping stones on the upper surface. Traditionally they are meant to represent bales of woollen cloth but some funeral historians think they are based on the hoops that covered the hearses and over which a covering was draped.

Monumental masons, like Mossfords in Cardiff, have supplied the local community – and what was once the Empire – with gravestones over six generations. If you visited their workshops in the 1930s, you would see craftsmen working on headstones but their headgear would tell you who they were. Apprentices wore hats made from newspapers, tradesmen wore flat caps and the foreman or head craftsman wore a fedora hat that would not have been out of place on the sleek head of a bank manager.

Today, Mossfords cater for a multi-faith community. Islamic, Jewish and Chinese inscriptions are their stock in trade as well as Welsh and English ones. The exotic alphabets are very carefully copied from prepared texts onto stone. Mistakes are expensive and rare.

In the eighteenth century, there was a dynasty of stonemasons in the border area, above and to the east of Crickhowell. In those days, if you had status in life and you wanted a memorial to match then you might have ordered a Brute.

The Brutes essentially were three generations of outstanding artist-masons. Thomas worked from 1721, Aaron from 1760 and John from 1780: they were grandfather, father and son respectively.

Liz Pitman, a keen amateur historian, has made a study of their work and showed us a number of churches where the Brutes' memorials were to be found. We started off in Llanbedr at St Peter's church. This was the Brutes' home village. Here we saw the distinctive thumbprint that distinguishes one Brute from another. Thomas, the grandfather used a curving line on the word AGED that linked the A with the D in a copper-plate style. He also used a tulip flower motif on his stones, but the image that captivated us the most was his portrayal of angels. Happy, chubby faces that looked just a little mischievous became a Brute calling card.

A friendly, convivial Brute angel.

Aaron, the father, often used an urn or basket of flowers at the bottom of his ledgers and gravestones. His son, John used a flower border down the side of his memorials and, like his father and grandfather, would sometimes sign off with his name on a cartouche, or at the bottom right-hand corner of the stone – just as an artist signs a painting.

Driving through the steep and narrow winding lanes around Llanthony Abbey, we eventually found Partrishow church, probably the prettiest little church in Wales. It is usually celebrated for its beautifully carved wooden rood screen but it houses a great collection of Brute monuments too. Some are on the walls and some on the floor of the church. One of the hallmarks of a Brute is the use of colour. Protected inside a church, crimsons, blues and golds still shine brightly enough despite the 200 years that have elapsed since they were first applied to the angels, flowers and scrolls that this talented family created. The colours were made from vegetable dyes from secret recipes that were kept in the family Bible.

Under a carpet we found a ledger stone signed by Thomas Brute, *fecit*, (maker). It was dedicated to Elizabeth Jenkins 1723. Many of their customers would have been, as Liz put it, the middling sort: independent farmers, country

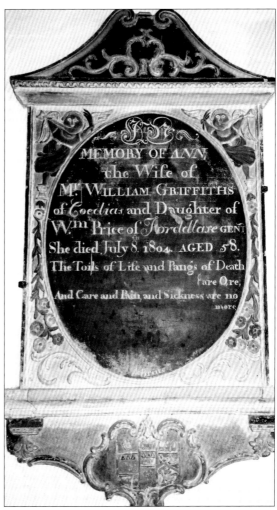

A coloured Brute memorial in Partrishow Church.

lawyers and innkeepers. Many of them wanted to have the word 'Gent' inscribed after their names. There was one memorial with a coat of arms prominently placed on its base, but research has determined it to be pure fantasy. The Brutes were obviously happy to indulge their clients and their customers' memorials might even be described as being on the jolly side. One stone has a pair of smiling angels blowing trumpets which one observer has likened to yards of ale.

Llangattock Church, on the west bank of the River Usk, has a number of Brutes decorating a wall by its bell tower. Here, we saw that what had seemed to be a collection of slate stones supporting the Brute designs was flaking a little. Upon examination of these imperfections, we saw that these stones were actually a painted sandstone and not slate, as the black finish had suggested. It hardly detracted from the charm and beauty of the work of the Brute family. Liz Pitman has recorded by photography and documentation scores of Brutes. Their memorials are spread through a number of parishes and Liz is keen to make a record of as many as she can locate. Many of them are fading now, but they do represent a very important and unique Welsh school of design, so conservation is vital.

Chapter Seven

Grave Stories from North Wales

THE RHIWLAS GAMBLER – LLANFOR

The hamlet of Llanfor is situated just outside Bala town. An unusual mausoleum with a pyramid-shaped roof in the churchyard there provides evidence that the Egyptians were not the only people to build their final resting-places years before they needed them. R. J. Lloyd Price built this miniature temple of death for himself while he was still only in his forties. The epitaph reads:

As to my latter end I go
To seek my jubilee
I bless the good horse Bendigo
Who built this tomb for me.

Richard John Lloyd Price 1887

R.J. was a gambler, and in 1887 he laid a substantial wager on Bendigo who won the Jubilee Stakes at Kempton Park. With his winnings, R.J. built the mausoleum. He wanted the building consecrated, and called on the Bishop of St Asaph to bless it for him. After the Bishop had inspected the inscription, he declined to consecrate the tomb because it was built on the proceeds of gambling, of which he strongly disapproved. R.J. was more than a match for his clerical critic and promptly replaced the offending inscribed stones with plain ones. The Bishop paid a second visit and this time he duly consecrated the building as requested. As soon as he was out of the way, R.J. promptly replaced the original, inscribed stones bearing their witty gambler's couplet.

The Gambler's Mausoleum at Llanfor.

R.J.'s ancestral home, Rhiwlas, has been in the family for centuries. Their good fortune dates from the time of Rhys ap Meredith, who was Standard Bearer to Henry Tudor at the Battle of Bosworth in 1485. As the family were on the winning side, they prospered mightily. In R.J.'s time the property extended to 120,000 acres in North Wales, and included various business enterprises including farming, slate quarrying, brickworks, brushworks, mineral-water bottling and fuller's earth.

R.J. had a lively sense of humour, and founded a social organisation which he called the Zigzag Club. The Members entertained themselves by playing cricket all day and billiards all night.

Dogs also had a prominent place in R.J.'s full and varied life. It is claimed that he devised and organised the first Sheep Dog Trials. Certainly, he kept up to 100 working dogs at one time, and thought highly enough about them to create a canine cemetery. R.J.'s great grandson, Robin Price, took us through some rough country before we located it. In that canine cemetery, we found a stone dedicated to Gather, the four-legged secretary of the Zigzag Club. His epitaph reads:

Ever answered to his master's call
Save once – the once for all.

Robin evidently shares R.J.'s great love of dogs, as he said that Gather's epitaph always brings tears to his eyes. A neighbouring stone commemorates a dog called Comedy:

Dearest of Retrievers accidentally shot
By her heartbroken master

Sad as he was, Comedy was probably even more upset. The Prices are obviously a sentimental family with a flair for choosing appropriate names for their dogs!

R.J. also had a literary gift and wrote *Dogs' Tales Wagged* and the unputdownable *Rabbits for Profit and Powder.*

R.J.'s beloved wife, Evelyn, shared many of his interests. She was well known for driving her coach pulled by four strawberry roans into Bala and then distributing food and other gifts to the poor. One fateful day, as she was returning from the town and making her way up the drive, a bird flew out of some bushes and startled the horses. They panicked and overturned the coach which crashed into the adjacent ravine. All four horses were so badly hurt that they had to be destroyed, and Evelyn herself died as a result of her injuries soon after the accident. She was laid to rest in the Bendigo Tomb.

R.J. consoled himself with work, and one of the enterprises that absorbed most of his attention between 1900 and 1910 was his Royal Welsh Whisky Distillery at nearby Frongoch. His ambition was to produce a pure malt of the highest possible quality. Such fine spirit took many years to mature, which meant that the distillery had nothing to sell to meet its expenses. Eventually, the enterprise folded. Meanwhile, R.J.'s business mistakes, excessive gambling and expensive recreational pursuits meant that the family estates had shrunk from 120,000 down to 30,000 acres.

The Government added to his problems by requisitioning the Frongoch Distillery premises for the incarceration of Irish Nationalists. A few years later, in 1916, German PoWs were imprisoned there – no doubt intoxicated by dreams of freedom, rather than by thoughts of R.J.'s pure malt Welsh whisky.

In 1923, at the age of 81, R.J. finally joined Evelyn in the tomb for which Bendigo's success had paid. R.J.'s great grandson, Robin Price, has no plans to join them there, preferring to be cremated and to have his ashes scattered on the land via a muck-spreader: a process which he hopes will do a lot of people a lot of good.

The mausoleum bought by Bendigo the race horse.

James Hannett's grave. He died aged eleven.

There are five distinctive slate gravestones in this Anglesey churchyard, four of them bearing an anchor and mooring-chain design above the name of a ship: the *Clio*.

The *Clio*, officially logged as an industrial training ship, was really a kind of floating borstal. She was moored in the Menai Straits from 1877 until 1920, overlooked by Llandegfan from the island side, and Bangor from the mainland. Twenty-nine names are inscribed on those solemn slates: the names of boys from the *Clio* who died either on board their grim vessel, or at sea later. The first stone commemorates James Hannett. Shockingly, he died aged only eleven.

In a circle, around the top of the stone, Victorian religiosity had seen fit to add the sanctimonious words:

 Those that seek me early shall find me.

During the following week, an inquest on Hannett was held at the Gazelle Inn, Garth Ferry. It was ascertained that he had fallen from a height of 70 feet (23 metres). The jury returned a verdict of accidental death. Hannett had been on board for only five weeks.

The boys aboard the *Clio* tended to have backgrounds as orphans, severely disadvantaged and impoverished children – or delinquents. Some, like Hannett, had been sent there from as far afield as Manchester and consequently, they had no-one to stand up for them against the authorities, or against the bullying of older boys. There was an official inspection of the ship on 27th May, 1882. Among its findings, it was stated that:

> The boys are small in size and young for a training ship, though nominally over twelve years of age. The situation of the *Clio* is stormy and exposed, too much so for the class of boys dealt with.

The fifth stone records – like a clinical list of casualties after a disaster – the names of eleven *Clio* boys, who died in different ways on different occasions. The list is headed by thirteen-year-old William Crook, who died on January 9th,

1905. A report on his particular tragedy contained this statement:

> A boy met his death as the result of concussion of the brain – the result of violence by other boys.

We looked into his case in depth with the help of Rev. John Gilliebrands, Vicar of Llandegfan Church, in whose shadow the *Clio* boys lie. He directed us to Bangor Museum, where we were able to pursue the story further. Among the exhibits there, we found one of the lifebelts from the *Clio* – a material link with the boys: something they would have seen every day. The Museum also provided us with extracts from the *North Wales Chronicle*. One was dated February 16th, 1906. It was headed:

Eleven *Clio* boys – who died long before their time.

Sad Death of a Clio Boy –
Alleged to be due to Bullying –
Coroner's Inquiry.

The gist of the report was that young Crook had been assaulted by older boys, who caused the fatal head injuries, one of these being 'a bruise the size of a half-crown on the boy's forehead'. After only fifteen minutes' retirement, the Coroner's jury returned a verdict of Death by Misadventure.

At the time, Captain Langdon, who was in charge of the *Clio*, said that his punishment book showed a list of 34 bullying incidents over a period of six weeks – as compared with only nine in any previous similar period since he had been in command of the *Clio*.

The attendant press publicity in Wales and beyond attracted Government attention to the plight of boys on Industrial Training Ships like the *Clio*. Too little, too late, for William Crook, but conditions did improve marginally for his shipmates. His assailants, meanwhile, were transferred to other vessels.

An editorial from the *Chronicle*, widely read in Bangor and North Wales – and always a stalwart defender of the people in charge of the *Clio* – included this comment:

> Bangorians will hope that the ship will pursue the even tenor of her way, and long continue to do the good work in the Menai Straits where she forms so striking a feature, and whence she sends forth her sons to swell the ranks of British sailors, both mercantile and naval.

Before the matter ended, there was a final Home Office Report, which more or less exonerated the senior ranks of the Clio – and no further questions were asked. An anonymous, bureaucratic hand signed off that last Report with these drily matter-of-fact words:

All's well that ends well.

THE GYPSY KING – LLANGELYNIN

A Gypsy King's grave. Who lies beside him?

Abram Wood is reputedly the Patriarch of the Welsh Gypsies, among whom the Wood family are still prominent today. The following entry comes from the Parish Burial Register of Llangelynin, a church so precariously perched on the edge of the coast that it is almost in the sea. The entry is dated 12th November, 1799: *Abram Wood a travelling Gypsy* ('Gypsy' was actually crossed out in the copperplate script in the Register and replaced with the word 'Egyptian').

Abram clearly was regarded as a bit of an outsider, yet his grave lies in a place of honour right by the church door – so he was evidently held in great respect and affection. The stone itself is not very informative. A plain rectangular slab, it is inscribed with two sets of initials:

 A.W.
1800

Although Abram's burial is recorded for 1799, it would seem that his stone was not laid over him until the following year. However, another set of initials to the left of his, raise an intriguing question:

 R.W.
1774

Who was the mysterious R.W. ? Various suggestions have been offered by gypsy genealogists, some based on a Parish Birth Register recording the baptism of

Abram's son, Solomon, by his wife, Sarah. The Gypsies have great respect for Bible stories and biblical traditions. The biblical Abram, who later became Abraham, was married to his half-sister Sarah. Her name signifies 'Princess' and our Abram Wood was known as a Gypsy King. The biblical Sarah died over twenty years before her husband, Abraham the Patriarch, and the mysterious R.W. who lies beside Abram Wood died over twenty years before he did. Is it possible that our Abram's wife was originally christened with a name beginning with R, but in order to forge a symbolic link between her Abram and the biblical one, she chose to be known as Sarah because she was the Gypsy King's consort. If not, R.W. is buried in mystery as well as in the earth.

Abram's appearance has come down through oral tradition. His family maintain that he wore a tri-corned hat, a tailcoat with half-crowns for buttons, and a waistcoat with buttons made from shillings. He also wore two gold rings. Like many of his people, he had a good eye for horses, and always rode a thoroughbred, which he referred to as a blood horse.

He seems to have moved to Wales from Somerset, attracted by the good fishing in the rivers in the Machynlleth area, especially the River Dovey. Like other gypsies of the period, Abram and his people were itinerant, seasonal farm-workers, but they were also skilled as wagon builders, wood-carvers and fishermen. Their Bohemian liveliness broke the monotonous routine of the hard life on eighteenth-century upland farms. The Woods were talented musicians, especially with harps and fiddles, and this provided them with additional income as well as helping to connect them positively with the community.

The Gypsy Lore Society, experts on Romany life and history, have noted that because Abram's people were relatively isolated in the Welsh mountains, the Woods retained a very old and pure form of their Romany language. One of the remote farms where Abram frequently worked was Hafod Taliadau, and it was here, while working in a barn with animals, that he collapsed and died. He was a very old man – and tradition suggests that he might even have ended his life as a centenarian.

It is appropriate that a man with such a passion for horses was carried by them to his final resting-place. A bier, harnessed to two powerful horses – one at each end – brought him down to Llangelynin Church on his last journey. That bier now hangs on the north wall of the nave, within sight of Abram's grave beside the door.

The bier that carried Abram to his grave.

Part of Gypsy belief was that the dead person's caravan – his *vardo* – along with all his possessions had to be disposed of by fire. The underlying reasoning behind this idea was that whatever curse, or evil fortune, had beset the dead man had to be cleansed with flames.

Throughout Mid and North Wales, there are secret, unmarked burial sites, known only to traditional Gypsies. It was the custom for them to dispose of their people in this way, in the belief that the bodies of the dead were reuniting with nature, while their souls went on to a new life with God. By contrast, conventional Christian thought in Abram's time focussed on death as a long sleep prior to resurrection. The descendants of those hidden Gypsies still visit the areas where their ancestors lie. These places are sacred to the Romany mind.

Their Names Live On

SIR CLOUGH WILLIAMS ELLIS – PORTMEIRION

He strove at Portmeirion and elsewhere to give some of his ideas physical expression.
He fought for beauty – that strange necessity.

Those words are on a memorial tablet to Sir Clough at his Italianate fantasy village at Portmeirion, but they weren't meant to be there. His family had worshipped for generations at Llanfrothen, but Sir Clough was an outspoken agnostic, so when his commemorative plaque was prepared for the church wall, the parishioners rejected it because of his irreligious views. A home had to be found for it somewhere, and it was installed in the Portmeirion Dome. This amazing structure had begun life as a huge fireplace, which had been salvaged from a Cheshire mansion. Appropriately, the plaque now looks down on an art gallery inside the Dome, featuring the work of former Welsh Artist of the Year, Rob Piercey.

Ninety-five-year-old Sir Clough's dying wish in 1978 was that following cremation his ashes should be fired off in a rocket. We were told that those ashes were kept by the family instead, so his final request never took off. To honour his memory, we decided to fire off our own rocket on his behalf, in the belief that if there was anything Out There, they ought to know about Sir Clough and Portmeirion. As co-author Lionel is President of the British UFO Research Association, and co-author Richard is a member of the Ducati Appreciation Society, we duly lit Sir Clough's memorial rocket together. It shot off into the heavens and exploded in a riot of noise and colour, startling our Dad's Army film crew!

So why was Abram Wood, a Gypsy King, buried in a country churchyard, and marked with a stone? There are no quick or easy answers, but it hints at his role as a bridge between his people and the settled community. His position by the church door may also symbolise his function as a cultural stepping-stone.

SLATE STORIES – FROM BETHESDA TO LLANDEGAI

The essential Welsh stone is slate, and in the north the great industry was quarrying. On the slabs cut from the bedrock for use as tombstones, the language of the bards was often carved. At Pentyr Church, west of Bethesda, J. Elwyn Hughes, a historian with a special interest in the structural rules of Welsh poetry, helped us to analyse the inscription on the grave of Robert Jones. Robert was a 16-year-old labourer at Penrhyn Quarry, Bethesda, who was brutally murdered by a workmate. The boy's epitaph takes the form of an *englyn*, a sophisticated yet popular form of poem dating back hundreds of years. It is arranged in four lines, each containing 10, 6, 7 and 7 syllables respectively. It has to have no more than thirty syllables in all. The scheme is further enhanced by rules concerning alliteration, assonance and rhyme, and *englynion* don't translate into English without a struggle! Robert Jones was murdered in 1862 and his grave takes the form of a chest-tomb in the centre of the churchyard. This is approximately what his translated *englyn* says:

 Death did not take him in the ordinary way.
It wasn't old age – but a man – that took his life.

Llandegai churchyard.

Both Robert and his suspected killer were employed by Lord Penrhyn at the biggest slate quarry in the world, the profits of which paid for his Lordship's castle: a ponderous, colossal fantasy built on the blood and sweat of those who hewed the stone to make roofing slates for most of the cities in Britain. In its heyday, the quarry employed 3000 workers, and over the years fatal accidents accounted for 400 of them.

Llandegai Church is only a short walk from Penrhyn Castle, and the church contains the ornately decorated tomb of Richard Pennant, Baron Penrhyn, the entrepreneur who developed and expanded the slate industry. Amongst the hyperbolic praise on his white marble memorial are these words:

He. . . improved the condition of the peasantry,
exciting them to habits of industry
by employment . . .

It would be interesting to know what the excited peasants thought of their master – so we went out to look for one!

This was no easy task, as nature was successfully reclaiming her territory at the back of the church. Thorns, tenacious roots, spiny shrubs and tangled branches obscured the graves and made our task almost impossible. But eventually we found the stone we were looking for. This formed the top of a low chest tomb, on which we read:

Here lies, in hope of a joyful resurrection,
the body of Robert Williams
A single man, late quarryman, who departed this life
On the 6th day of February 1792
Aged 23 years.

His *englyn* followed, and this is roughly how it translates:

The minute for my life to end
Was registered and noted.
Cold body under stones – a crushing load –
I met my death.

Robert was one of the first to die amid the hazards of the quarry, and, amazingly, the heavy slab that fell and killed him there is the ***same one*** that now covers him and carries his memorial and *englyn*. (See page 47)

That same cemetery at Llandegai bears witness to the indescribable pain and loss suffered by parents in those days of ever-present infant mortality, referred to in Chapter Five.

On the south side of the church is a gravestone commemorating the Roberts children:

Anne	1843	Aged 3
Marg	1846	Aged 4
Rob.	1846	Aged 5
Hugh	1850	Aged 6
Cath.	1850	Aged 3

Just a few yards away, another stricken family recorded the names of their lost children, and revealed the general tendency for bereaved parents at that time to give a later child the same name as an older brother or sister who had died. Tragically, these re-named children often died too:

Eliz.	1853	Aged 4
Eliz.	1857	Aged 3
John	1862	Aged 2
John	1866	Aged 3

For the grimmest statistic, the reader can visit a grave in St Anne's churchyard in Bethesda and see a list of nine children from one family who were all typhoid victims.

While scrambling around in the undergrowth at Llandegai, we stumbled across a small, lost and abandoned grave-marker – the slate was about the size of a baby, and contained these details:

 Gwen Rowland
1767
Aged 1 day

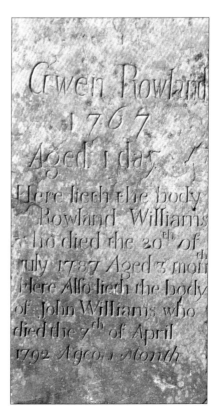

We carried her small stone out of the darkness and rested it against the east wall of the church, facing the morning light.

On a happier note, just by the west door of the church, is a stone to Grace Rowland, a midwife, who died in 1852 at the age of 71. Her inscription proudly records that she brought 705 children *into* the world.

Grace Rowland's proud record is inscribed on her grave.

DAVID LLOYD GEORGE – LLANYSTUMDWY

The First Earl Lloyd George of Dwyfor, Prime Minister from 1916 – 1922, is buried on the bank of the River Dwyfor which runs through the village. Sir Clough Williams-Ellis designed the grave, which takes the form of a huge boulder resting on cobblestones in the centre of a simple oval enclosure. Jonah Jones, the sculptor, inscribed Lloyd George's name and dates on two oval slate plaques. The grave has been classified as a World Heritage Site.

Chapter Eight

Grave Stories from Cardiff to Merthyr

Their Names Live On

GUTO NYTH BRÂN – LLANWYNNO

On the steep slopes of Llanwynno above Mountain Ash stands the picturesque church of St Gwynno. The most famous grave in its churchyard is dedicated to a runaway success: it bears the name Griffith Morgan. He was a phenomenal runner, said to be able to keep up with the hounds, win races against horses, catch birds in

flight – and once he outran a hare and caught it. The upright stone that celebrates his life was actually erected 100 years after his death in 1737. At the foot of this 1837 stone lies the original horizontal slab inscribed with a broken heart – and that's the key to this story.

Griffith was born in 1700 at Nyth Brân Farm near Porth in the Rhondda Valley. His friends called him Guto, and so he was widely known as Guto Nyth Brân. So successful was he as a runner that it became difficult to find opponents who were willing to race against him. Then, when he was 37, he was challenged by an athletic rival calling himself Prince of Bedwas. They agreed to run a twelve-mile race from Newport to Bedwas near Caerphilly.

Guto won easily, and finished well ahead of Prince.

Tragedy struck as his enthusiastic well-wishers gathered round to congratulate him. Hearty blows on his back proved too much for Guto. The last, fatal, congratulatory slap was delivered by his sweetheart, Siân o'r Siop. It apparently brought on the heart seizure – aggravated by exhaustion – from which he died: hence the broken heart symbol carved on his original grave.

His fame, however, never died. In 1958, the Nos Galan Races were inaugurated in Guto's honour. The best British sprinters came to Mountain Ash and ran in the New Year through midnight. In the fifties, these celebrated runners competed over a 100-yard course, while local athletes and enthusiasts took part in a four-mile race around the town.

Since the1980s, the main race has been run from the church at Llanwynno over a distance of five kilometres. A sports celebrity – whose identity is kept secret until the last moment – lays a wreath on Guto's grave, and then 200 men and women race downhill towards Guto's statue in the main street of Mountain Ash.

FALL FROM THE SKY – CARDIFF

In 1896, Cardiff hosted a Great Exhibition dedicated to Industry, Science and Art. It was a huge event with many entertainments, during which fourteen-year-old Mademoiselle Albertina died trying to please the crowds.

Brave woman, yet in years a child,
Dark death closed here
Thy heavenward flight.
God grant thee, pure and undefiled,
To reach at last the light of light.

Those are the words at the bottom of her fine white marble gravestone in Cathays Cemetery, Fairoak Road.

Albertina arrived in Cardiff alone on Sunday, 12th July, with her meagre possessions wrapped in a brown-paper parcel. She managed to find a room in a newly-built terraced house at 9, Pearson Street, but the landlady was suspicious because of her lack of luggage, and Albertina was asked to leave a day later. She wandered the unfamiliar streets of Cardiff until midnight, and then located her employer, Monsieur Gaudron, a French showman, and his wife at 19, Edward Street. They made up a makeshift sofa-bed for their young assistant. Next day, they set off for the Exhibition site at what is now Cathays Park to prepare the daring act that was their speciality. Gaudron had a hot-air balloon in which his assistant ascended in harness, and then parachuted from the rising balloon, landing nearby – if everything went according to plan.

At 7.30 p.m. on Tuesday, 21st July, Albertina, dressed in a fashionable sailor-suit, took off attached to the balloon. The writers suspect that the balloon must normally have been anchored by a cable, enabling Gaudron to raise and lower it so that he could repeat his shows. Contemporary reports refer to strong winds that day and a very rapid ascent. A vulnerable young girl like Albertina would have felt obligated to carry out her master's instructions, even though conditions were obviously hazardous.

She had precious little, if any, experience of parachuting and ballooning, so when the strong winds played havoc with her descent, Albertina was at the mercy of the elements and was blown out to sea. A Penarth Coastguard saw her descending down the Rumney River, with her parachute half in and half out of the water. Three small boats put out at once to try to rescue her, but when they reached the spot where she had last been seen there was no sign of Albertina or her parachute. A brave local man, James Dunn, saw her being dragged for a 100 metres or so along the river, and swam out to help her, but when he reached the spot, she had vanished.

The incident caught the public imagination, and was fuelled by frequent reports in the *Echo* newspaper. These were the headlines for Wednesday, 22nd July:

Lady Parachutist's Fate
No tidings after many hours

On Thursday, 23rd July:

All hope abandoned
Searching for the body

The *Echo* even suggested that fumes from the Dowlais Works had rendered her unconscious as her parachute took her over their chimneys. Regarding Monsieur Gaudron, it said that he was much troubled but was strong in the belief that his pupil had been picked up. Adverse comment was rife that she had been allowed to go up in such a strong wind, and that no arrangement had been made for a tugboat to be on the look-out for her.

The headline on Friday, 24th July declared:

Body discovered in Usk

We filmed the spot where Albertina's body was found amid the slippery boulders and treacherous mud on the east bank of the River Usk, by the entrance to Newport. The high water had brought the body there, and left it pathetically stranded as the tide ebbed away. When she was carried to Nash Church, her harness and costume were intact: the brave girl must have found the strength and presence of mind to release the parachute that was dragging her down, but had then failed to swim to the shore. Those who found her said that she looked as if she was only asleep.

One result of the tragedy was that Albertina's real name, age and background became known, thanks to the diligent investigations of local reporters. She was really Louisa Maud Evans, fourteen-and-a-half years old, and from Bristol. She had run away from her foster parents there, and joined a party of travelling show people: an environment where few questions were asked.

During the inquest, Gaudron was censured for carelessness and lack of judgement in allowing so young and inexperienced a person to make such a perilous ascent. The Coroner, commenting on its being Louisa's first parachute jump, said: 'As to its being the first time, well everybody must go up the first time.'

To which the Foreman replied: 'Rather a dangerous place, sir, in Cardiff for a first time.'

The Coroner then answered: 'Yes, but she didn't carry out the instructions of Gaudron. She was told to drop over the Infirmary. If she had carried out his instructions in that respect, she would probably have landed, not in the water.' It seems astonishing to us in the 21st century, that no one was particularly concerned about how young she was. Some reports also claimed that she had first met Gaudron in the West Country and had actually jumped before coming to Cardiff. Whether she had or not, the Coroner's formal verdict was that Louisa had died from accidental drowning.

The sympathetic citizens of Cardiff were heartbroken over the untimely and patently avoidable death of such a courageous girl as Albertina. Their Public Subscription paid for her funeral and an expensive memorial stone – which explains why her grave is in Cathays Cemetery. Mr Whitworth, the Cemetery Inspector, inured to grief and death by his years of professional experience, reflected that sympathy in his Burial Register entry in 1896. Against Louisa Maud/Albertina's name he wrote: 'Poor little soul'. He also made the cryptic entry: 'It ought to be.' Did he mean: 'It ought to have been Gaudron'?

In his Element – Merthyr Tydfil

Most modern gravestones are made to a pattern and don't really reflect the personality of the departed. Cefn Coed Cemetery, Merthyr Tydfil, contains a modern stone with a difference.

The inscription on David Robert Flint's grave is written in a clockwise spiral with an ammonite in the middle – because David was a geologist. An ammonite is an extinct marine mollusc, now found in a distinctive fossil form.

Ann, David's widow, told us that she had chosen those words because they were not a religious family, but wanted a symbol from nature which would reflect David's main interest.

David was very enthusiastic about rock formations and his work had taken the family to Africa for ten years. They returned to Merthyr to care for elderly relatives and to educate their three daughters in Wales.

David suddenly developed an acute sore throat that developed into the life-threatening condition known as epiglottitis, an illness that causes severe swelling and cuts off the air supply. Tragically, David died before effective treatment could be administered.

Because David and Ann had always been very close, she wants her memorial – when the time comes – to be just like his. Accordingly, she is keeping a section of the same

David Robert Flint's geological epitaph.

ammonite that has been set into David's stone. She also plans to use an identical type of circular epitaph, but her spiral inscription will be anti-clockwise – a mirror image of David's.

There is an interesting precedent for geologists attracting unusual memorials relevant to their profession. Thanks to Archbishop Whateley's *Common-Place Book*, we have this elegy dedicated to the late Dr Buckland, an outstanding Victorian geologist:

Mourn, ammonites, mourn o'er his funeral urn . . .

. . . If we hew him a rocky sepulchre
He'll rise and break the stones,
And examine each stratum which lies around,
For he's quite in his element underground.

If with mattock and spade his body we lay
In the common alluvial soil,
He'll start up and snatch these tools away
Of his own geological toil.
In a stratum so young the Professor disdains
That embedded should lie his organic remains . . .

The Iron Rebel – Aberafan

His name was Richard Lewis – but that's not the name he's remembered by.

In 1831 Merthyr Tydfil experienced the most serious uprising in nineteenth-century Britain. It was the result of agitation for parliamentary reform and a protest against the untrammelled power of the local Iron Masters. Richard Lewis was a 23-year-old miner known as Dic Penderyn: he was the only rioter to be officially executed – but he hadn't killed anyone.

Merthyr was *the* iron town. Its phenomenal growth and prosperity were built on iron – but prices for the metal fell drastically and wages were cut in consequence. The iron master of the day, William Crawshay II, was not especially anti-union, just anti-disturbance.

Distress in the town usually started at the infamous Court of Requests. Slashed wages left many iron workers unable to meet their essential rent and food bills. Creditors went to the Court of Requests, which then organised the seizure of debtors' goods in order to settle their unpaid bills.

In May 1831, some bailiffs from this Court went to Penderyn, a nearby village, where a haulier named Lewis Lewis lived. Their summary action led to his emergence as one of the leaders of the riots.

In accordance with their normal tactics, the bailiffs took some of Lewis Lewis's possessions and duly returned to the Court. The people in Penderyn protested vehemently, and their protests soon spread to other parts of Merthyr Tydfil. Indignant demonstrations took place wherever people had bought seized property from the court. The protests seemed to take on a life of their own, growing, spreading and becoming angrier all the time.

Hungry protesters took up a chant of 'Bread and cheese!' like a mantra of rebellion, and advanced grimly on the Castle Inn.

On June 3, 1831, (during the reign of King William IV) close on 10,000 people caused mayhem in the town. Inside the Inn were the Iron Masters and the Special Constables who were protecting them. Some Argyll and Sutherland Highlanders were called from Brecon to protect these worthies. Soldiers fired into the crowd. 24 people were killed, and 16 soldiers wounded, some quite badly.

One of the soldiers, Donald Black, was stabbed in the thigh with a bayonet.

Dic Penderyn was accused of that attack on the soldier. A barber, James

Abbot, testified that he had witnessed the action at the Castle Inn. He swore that Dic had wrestled with Black for possession of the musket. Lewis won the struggle for it and stuck the bayonet into Black's thigh. Abbot said that that violent thrust had made him indignant and caused him to take particular note of the incident.

But Black himself said that although he saw Dic nearby, he could not swear that he had carried out the attack on him. 'I cannot say I saw him stab me: he stood near the place where I was stabbed.'

The judge, passing sentence, said to Dic: 'It is upon your head that the responsibility must rest for the blood which has fallen.'

Despite Black's honest and objective testimony, and the fact that Dic had not killed anyone, he was condemned to death. He was taken to the County Gaol in Cardiff and hanged. With his dying breath, Dic cried out, 'Injustice!'

A local JP of the time wrote, in a recently discovered letter, that it would be better if Dic's body was not buried in Merthyr Tydfil as his friends might view the occasion as an excuse for another riot; so Dic's remains were sent to the place of his birth, Aberafan. His body was quietly slipped into unconsecrated ground there, as he was, in the eyes of the establishment, a convicted criminal. The carter who conveyed Dic's body from Cardiff to Aberafan expressed his admiration and sympathy for Dic. According to tradition, he wished to be buried beside his hero when his own time came. Today Dic Penderyn is honoured as a working-class martyr, and held up as a hero in books and plays on the Merthyr Tydfil riots. Like the carter, people can readily identify with him, and the cause for which he stood.

Current thought among historians suggests that *Lewis* Lewis was the real leader of the riot and that Dic Penderyn was just a 'foot soldier'. Maybe the wrong Lewis was put on trial – it isn't likely that the nervous authorities in 1831 would be too bothered about whom they decided to make an example of.

Richard Lewis's memorial stone.

The Iron Master – Vaynor

Mid-nineteenth-century Iron Masters still ruled when Robert Crawshay took over, but it was under his inauspicious leadership that the iron works closed, and his relationships with both his family and his labour force were catastrophically damaged.

This fourth Iron King was a lover of nature and made a great point of selecting the specific tree from which his coffin was to be constructed. He is buried fourteen feet below ground at Vaynor Churchyard, and his grave is surrounded by sturdy iron railings. There is no immediate danger of excavation because his huge red granite tomb-slab weighs eleven tons. Thirteen powerful horses dragged it all the way up from Radyr Quarry: a distance of over 30 kilometres.

Robert's poignant epitaph:

 God Forgive Me

has been interpreted as meaning that he was sorry for the way that he had treated his workers. Another theory is that he was a pious man who had repented before he died. But neither of these explanations is true.

Robert Thompson Crawshay was a strange mixture of intelligence, sensitivity and stubbornness. At his worst he could also be vindictive, aggressive and cantankerous. Robert was the eldest son of his father's second marriage, and had never been expected to inherit the Iron Works. His half-brother, William, who was the heir apparent, died crossing the Severn Estuary, and Robert's father appointed him in preference to Francis – who should have been next in line.

In 1860, Robert was broken by a crippling illness and profound deafness, which altered his whole character and made him heavily dependent on his daughter, Rose Harriette, or Trotty, as she was called. He made her promise never to leave him, but the strain of looking after such a difficult invalid proved too much. Trotty fell in love, married and left home.

Spitefully, Crawshay added a codicil to his will disinheriting her children. It was this bitter realisation of what he had done to his grandchildren, which led to the much misunderstood inscription on his tomb-slab.

Crawshay's prayer for forgiveness.

DR JOSEPH PARRY – PENARTH

A graceful memorial in St Augustine's churchyard in Penarth honours this great Welsh musician's memory. When Parry died on February 17th, 1903, his widow instructed the stonemasons to carve one special line on that memorial:

He is watching and waiting for me.

Joseph's fine marble monument is crowned with a harp. Its carved strings are mute, but its unmistakable form reminds every visitor who sees it of the unparalleled contribution which he made to music throughout Wales and the world.

Born in Merthyr Tydfil in a mid-terrace, worker's cottage on May 21st, 1841, Joseph Parry began his working life as a pit boy. After a year, he had transferred to the Iron Works, where he did menial tasks. His family then moved to Pennsylvania in America. From there he competed by mail in *eisteddfodau* in Wales. His work so impressed the adjudicators that they raised the necessary funds to bring Joseph back to Wales, where his prodigious musical gifts eventually took him to the Professorship of Music at Aberystwyth University. His talents as a prolific composer and writer of sacred songs led to the creation of numerous operas and over 700 hymns. His most famous and best-loved single work is the deeply moving melody *Myfanwy*, which brings comfort and solace to the bereaved at so many funerals.

Chapter Nine

Grave Stories from the Western Valleys to Carmarthen

BEAU NASH – SWANSEA & BATH

Of all of the celebrities of the eighteenth century few were more colourful than Richard Nash. Born in Swansea in 1674 he was more commonly known as Beau Nash.

To His remains consign one grateful Tear,
Of Youth the Guardian and of All the Friend.

Nash laid down the blueprint that turned a poor West country town, Bath, into the Las Vegas of the eighteenth century. It attracted royal visits, became fashionable, enhanced your position in the world if you went there – and its success was largely based on gambling.

Nash's father, who came from a well-established Pembroke family, owned a bottle factory in the docks area of Swansea. Richard Nash was educated at Carmarthen Grammar School and in 1691 he was sent to Jesus College, Oxford, to read Jurisprudence. He was later attached to the Inner Temple, London, but decided that the legal profession had little to attract him. He preferred gaming tables and organising social events. Mixing and skilfully wheedling his way up in society, young Nash managed to organise a pageant for King William the Third. Evidently, this met with royal approval and Nash was offered a knighthood by a grateful monarch. When Nash replied that he would be pleased to be a *pensionable* Knight of Windsor, he heard no further news from the palace.

Soon after, Richard Nash discovered that Bath might hold out some prospects for him. He travelled west and became an assistant to a Captain Webster, the Master of Ceremonies in the town. Nash helped to organise some celebrations and parties. When Webster died in a duel, Nash was voted into the M.C. role whereupon he took on the title of Master of Revels to boot. He was to bring fame, fortune and splendour to the town, beyond its wildest dreams.

Nash arranged subscriptions to balls, and regulated codes of dress and behaviour (once asking a booted squire at a genteel dance whether he'd forgotten to bring his horse with him) and policed his patch effectively, sorting out the problem of highwaymen at the approaches to Bath. His master plan was to develop gambling in an environment which he controlled and partly managed.

Social schedules were arranged for all well-heeled visitors. The day began with a service at Bath Abbey followed by the taking of the waters at the Pump Rooms. These were excavated more comprehensively in the next century to reveal the true extent of the Roman activities here. But in Nash's time it was enough to take the curative waters or to view the early morning bathers in the King's Bath. After which it was time to socialise and take refreshments. Today, it is still possible to enjoy this same environment where tea and cakes are served to modern tourists, and you can still sample the odorous, sulphurous waters if you wish. A servant in costume serves up glasses of the pungent water from an ornate fountain for those brave enough to try it – one of the present co-authors had three! Nash still presides over the Pump Room. He has a statue to himself at one end of the large salon. If you were to visit Bath in Nash's day you might have heard this about the town:

> Here is performed all the wanton dalliance imaginable, celebrated beauties, panting breasts and curious shapes almost exposed to public view. Languishing eyes, darting killing glances, tempting amorous postures attended by soft musick enough to provoke a vestal to forbidden pleasures.

Beau Nash's memorial tablet in Bath Abbey.

Richard, now Beau Nash, prospered and his vanity showed in his equipage. He had a grand coach drawn by six greys, a running footman, French horns and the grandest house in town. His home – once centre stage in his life – still stands in St John's Court but is now the Theatre Royal. Nash plainly enjoyed palatial, not to say spacious, surroundings. To maintain his lifestyle he employed women as debt collectors. They would charm or shame the guilty party into paying and some of these women were also Nash's consorts. His favourite was the deliciously named, Juliana Popjoy.

New gaming laws and the influence of the church were to curtail Nash's career, although it was a long one. He ruled the town for a remarkable fifty years before his own money began to run out and he had to move to more modest premises around the corner. Nash and Miss Popjoy retired to Saw Close, still a fine property and used today as a restaurant.

In his final years, Nash was reduced to selling off his possessions to keep himself in old age. When he died in 1761 he had no liquid assets and there was no cash for a funeral. The grateful town authorities did him proud in the end. With great pomp and ceremony he was buried at Bath Abbey. His remains lie below the floor of this beautiful structure and a memorial tablet on the south-facing wall displays his epitaph.

Juliana Popjoy was somewhat less fortunate. It was reported that with no income available, she had to return to her home village, where she spent the last few years of her life living in a hollowed-out tree.

Their Names Live On

THE EMMANUELS – PONTRHYDYFEN

During the 1960s, Ivor Emmanuel was a household name. He played leading roles in musicals and starred in network television shows. His most famous part was in the film *Zulu*, which also starred Stanley Baker and Michael Caine. Ivor, played the part of a South Wales Borderer in the Zulu Wars and led a rendition of *Men of Harlech* as fierce warriors attacked the mission post at Rorke's Drift. This was based on the real events surrounding one of the most stirring battles involving Welsh soldiers.

Tragically, war was to devastate Ivor's family in very different circumstances. When he was a young boy, his Pontrhydyfen home was hit by bombs ditched from an enemy aeroplane during the Second World War. Most of his family were wiped out and Ivor himself was lucky to survive.

Stan Pope, father of Mal Pope the songwriter and TV presenter, was an eye witness to those terrible events. At the time, Stan's family ran the local shop, R. Glyn Pope and Son . . . General Merchants. They lived and worked just a few doors up the street from the Emmanuels who used to call in and often bought Pope's Tea, *blended to suit the waters of the district.*

The district, like the rest of Britain, was at war and German planes flew over South Wales on their way to their principal targets. On the night of May 11th 1941, that war burst in on the village. Stan told us how he heard the Heinkel 111s flying overhead and that there was the sound of eighteen bombs exploding through the valley. His parents ran into his bedroom and told seventeen year old Stan and his younger brother Colin to hide under their bed. Then there was an ominous silence.

The Heinkels had been turned back by RAF fighters and one of the German planes had shed its bombs over the main street. It is thought that the pilot hoped his deadly cargo would fall onto the wooded slopes of the valley. Tragically, it fell onto Number 18, Morgan's Terrace.

Stan soon ran out onto the street. Crowds began to gather amongst the rubble and a lone policeman with a gas mask hung over his tunic tried to organise a rescue party to save the bombed-out householders. There was Ivor, his parents, Gretta and Steve, his uncle and grandfather and his sister, little Mair, to account for. Stan recalls that one of three spinster sisters who lived at Number 10 called to him. He went over and was beckoned inside and asked if he knew the little girl who was lying there. She was dying in terrible agony. Stan recognised her immediately as four-year-old Mair Emmanuel.

Ivor's parents and grandfather had been killed and a few days later most of the family were buried at Jerusalem Chapel. It stands on the steep slopes looking towards the monumental viaduct that bridges the valley. On the side of the grave etched in gold are these words

A gollodd eu bywydau drwy law gelyn
yn ystod rhyfel, ar Fai 1941
They lost their lives at the hands of the enemy
during the war, May 1941

Husband and Wife, Steve and Gretta lie here with their daughter, Mair.

The grandfather was buried in another plot. Ivor and his uncle survived and Ivor found fame in show business before retiring early to sunny Spain, where he still lives. Stan went on to serve in the Royal Navy and saw action during the war, but he has never erased the images of that night from his mind, and he remains now an uncompromising pacifist.

THE PILGRIMS' REST – LLANFIHANGEL ABERCOWYN

We trekked through several fields alongside the River Cowyn, near St Clears in search of hidden treasure, or that's what a grave historian would claim regarding these memorials. We had been given a hot tip by our good friend, sculptor and television adventurer, David Petersen, regarding six unusual-looking stones near his home and studio. After pushing on through some trees we came across the ruins of a church.

St Michael's was originally a twelfth-century Norman structure but was abandoned in 1848 because it was too remote.

There are hardly any visible graves here but those that remain are amongst the most intriguing we came across in the making of the television series. On the south side of the church are three ledgers, flat stones at ground level. Their headstones are approximately 40 cm high.

Mysterious medieval graves at St Michael's.

There are no written epitaphs on these stones, but the dead are represented pictorially. The craftwork is a mixture of the skilful and the crude and shows: Maltese crosses, cable decoration, circles within circles and primitive human outlines. Legend claims these three graves as being those of pilgrims and Wyn Evans, the Dean of St Davids, does not disagree.

The Dean told us that this church was on the pilgrim's route to St David's Cathedral. At low tide it was possible, claimed the Dean, to walk across the estuary and continue westwards to the cathedral city to visit the relics of Wales's patron saint. The pilgrims buried at Llanfihangel Abercowyn, were, according to the old story, short of food. They became so hungry that they instructed one of their number to kill the other two. Having despatched his friends, the third pilgrim pulled the final slab of stone over his own body and died of hunger himself.

In 1839, the middle grave was opened up and bones were found belonging to a young person. Among the skeletal remains were large scallop-shells, the symbol of a pilgrim, and in particular those who had visited the shrine at Santiago Compostella in Northern Spain.

Equestrian figure at St Michael's.

There are another three graves about 50 metres downhill from the pilgrims. Here two ledgers lie either side of a small rectangular stone. An equestrian figure resembling a Knight can be seen on the southernmost headstone. We thought this, in combination with the Maltese crosses might suggest a Knights Templar connection. But our research did not indicate that any warrior priests, or some such organisation, had operated this far west. There was a Templar House in the Gower but nothing in this area.

Most experts agree that it is probably a family grave of a Knight and his Lady. The middle stone has the feint form of a small girl on it suggesting the couple's daughter lies with them. This group might have been the landowners who were responsible for the foundation of the church. Their deaths are a mystery but they lie in graves which were almost certainly carved by the same hands as those which worked on the pilgrims' graves that share the site with them.

THE WEAVER RIOTER – PONTARDDULAIS

Daniel Lewis lies in Pontarddulais but the injustice he fought against could have sent him to Van Diemen's Land. It was then a seventeen-week journey to present day Tasmania, followed by hard labour: the penalty for taking part in the Rebecca Riots of the 1830s and 1840s. Daniel Lewis's epitaph is written in a Coelbren script, the alphabet of the ancient bards and says, in translation:

ᚻe loved his nation –
himself he was prepared to sacrifice.

Throughout rural west Wales there was poverty and hardship. The population had doubled and this placed a massive strain on resources. There was also the problem of the roads. Powerful landowners had set up trusts to improve roadways and handed the management of them over to agents. Farmers keen to obtain lime to fertilise their fields might have to pass through more than a dozen toll gates in as many miles on their way to a quarry.

In 1839, farmers began to riot in an area north of Narberth and the protests spread quickly. Toll gates were pulled down and smashed, but what distinguished these attacks were the costumes worn by the rioters. They dressed as women to disguise themselves and they were named after the biblical Rebecca from the book of Genesis XXIV, verse 60:

> And they blessed Rebecca, and said unto her, 'Thou art our sister, be thou the mother of thousands of millions, and let thy seed possess the gate of those which hate them.'

The destruction of the three gates near Pontarddulais were amongst the most serious acts of the Rebecca Rioters. Daniel Lewis, a weaver and self-educated reformer was involved with the group that operated in this area. He was also wooing Elizabeth, the daughter of the landlord of the Fountain Inn which overlooked the Bolgoed Gate. At the height of the riots, Elizabeth watched the action from her bedroom window and saw that Daniel, her lover, was clearly leading the rioters. His disguise must have been hurriedly applied that night. The event was one in which there were recriminations. Riots are often used to settle old scores and the Bolgoed Gate incident was no exception.

A local man, John Jones, who was known as a petty thief and drunkard had recently been evicted from a cottage by some farmers. He was also infatuated with Elizabeth and was jealous of Daniel Lewis, the weaver-poet, who had a talent for spinning words of love. Jones went to the authorities and fingered Daniel and others. He accused them of the destruction of the gates. Lewis and his friends were arrested. But Jones's wife who was fed up with his behaviour told the local constabulary that Jones could not possibly have seen what took place on the night in question as he was somewhere else at the time. None of the convictions could stand up to this new evidence, or lack of it; so all the men involved in the Bolgoed incident were freed.

Gopa Chapel stands on the land once occupied by Daniel Lewis's cottage-workshop. In its graveyard is a two-metre upright rectangular stone with a small pyramidal top to it. This is Daniel and Elizabeth's grave. They were the grandparents of the famous journalist and broadcaster, Wynford Vaughan Thomas, who often expressed his pride in having such spirited ancestors.

Daniel Lewis was a poet and his gravestone bears the assumed alphabet of ancient bards. Coelbren script was developed by stone mason, Iolo Morganwg, the founder of the modern *eisteddfod* as part of his re-interpretation of Welsh culture and history in the eighteenth century. Historian, Peter Stead, who took us to some of the key locations in this story expressed his view that new worlds are often born out of mythology and that modern society owes much to artisans like Daniel Lewis, who cherished the past and made a meaningful contribution to life in Wales . . . then and now.

Their Names Live On

RICHARD BURTON – PONTRHYDYFEN TO CELIGNY

Richard Burton's dramatic skills and his headline-grabbing marriage to Elizabeth Taylor made him the king of glamour and the toast of Wales throughout the 50s and 60s. They met in 1962 while filming *Cleopatra*, then the most expensive movie ever made. But their affair made them even more famous than the films in which they starred.

Burton was born at Number 2, Dan-y-Bont, Pontrhydyfen, a stone's throw from the towering viaduct that dwarfs the house, but he is buried in Celigny, Switzerland. A simple stone monolith stands over his grave with the simplest of inscriptions.

His coffin bears his real name, shared with his father, Richard Walter Jenkins. Burton's stage name was a tribute to his old English teacher.

When Richard Burton used to visit his family as a famous movie-star in Pontrhydyfen, he preferred to stay with his sister, Hilda. She had a small terraced house and hosted Richard and Elizabeth a number of times. Elizabeth insisted on staying in one of the bedrooms rather than going off to a posh hotel. Siân Owen, actress and niece of Richard, still uses the room that the megastars occupied. She showed us around the lilac-painted bedroom and pointed out that the bed is the same one that they used in the 1960s.

Richard Burton had actually arranged a burial plot in the cemetery at Jerusalem Chapel, Pontrhydyfen, for himself and Elizabeth, but they divorced and Richard spent more time at his home in Switzerland. He married his fourth wife, Sally, and Celigny, just a few minutes' drive from Geneva, became his main residence. He lived there initially to benefit from the advantages of Swiss tax laws.

Whenever he was struck by *hiraeth*(a longing for home in Wales), he would phone his sister, Hilda and persuade her to come over. We actually flew out to Switzerland while making the *Talking Stones* series to film Burton's grave. Whenever we asked ordinary people in Wales where they thought his final resting-place was, we were always told either Hollywood, London or the Rhondda. It was our mission to put the record straight and bring back the pictorial evidence.

When we called on his former home, a modern fifties-style, detached country house surrounded by an orchard, we made a cold call. The owners were friendly and invited us back the next day. In the meantime, we discovered the Café de la Gare: Richard's favourite watering hole where he and the owner enjoyed a few glasses of wine together. There is a corner of the bar that is hung with pictures of Richard and le Patron, Paul Filitoff, checking out the wine cellars. We had never seen these photographs in any tribute to Burton so we duly recorded them. They showed him in a relaxed environment with a friend, clearly enjoying himself.

Later the same day we visited the village cemetery. Dappled light fell on a few graves behind a pale blue iron gate.

Burton's plot was marked with a triangular-shaped rock about one and a half metres high. It bore only his name and the years of his birth and death. At the foot of the rock was a single white rose. Sally Burton had visited the site a couple of days before. We filmed the scene and returned to Celigny the next day to take a few shots of the house. Burton called his Swiss home Le Pays de Galles and the name-plate in wrought iron is still fixed on the garden wall.

The family who own the property today are artistically inclined and their daughter who was about fifteen years old played the violin for us while we filmed some interiors. The house was large and comfortable but rather modest for such a celebrity, we thought. Still, Burton was comfortable here most of the time. Six weeks before he died he phoned Hilda to plan his funeral. He decided to be buried in Celigny. The financial problems of coming home to Wales, his children and the media interest in Elizabeth Taylor were complicated, so he decided it would be easier on everyone if he stayed where he was.

When he died of a cerebral haemorrhage in 1984 he was buried according to his wishes entirely in red: red suit, red shirt, red socks – the lot.

Recently, his niece, Siân Owen, spoke with Elizabeth Taylor on the phone as they do from time to time. Just after her seventieth birthday, Elizabeth Taylor confirmed that she still intends to be buried in Pontrhydyfen – as originally planned by Richard Burton.

Chapter Ten

Flora and Fauna in Churchyards

Churchyards are older than cemeteries and their history and location gives them a special atmosphere. It is a mood created by something more than graves and dedications to the departed. There are trees and shrubs, velvet mosses, odd angles of stone, birds, small mammals, porches, gates and dry walls covered in ivy. These are living places where animals and plants feed and make their beds. Here, we can feel in touch with nature as well as with the past: a miniature landscape where nostalgia, solitude and a gentle respect for death allow you to enter a special haven. Graveyards are attractive to wildlife because they are usually undisturbed. Some are more overgrown than others, and some have been organised to fit in with the needs of the lawn-mower, but they are still home to many creatures and plants.

Natural fields and meadows have largely gone, vanquished by chemicals and agricultural machinery. But churchyards were cut from ancient pastures and have never been ripped up or sprayed with toxic liquids. Just one acre of churchyard may contain over 120 different examples of vegetation creeping around the gravestones.

Among graveyard flowers we encounter: moon-daisy, daisy (day's eye), nettles, dock, mosses, several different types of grass, celandine, buttercups, speedwells, vetch, clover, violets, and, occasionally, the small yellow wild-wallflower which has been seen growing 20 feet and more up church towers. Graveyards also provide sanctuary for escaped domestic or introduced flowers, such as roses from gardens of remembrance. Wild roses also decorate graveyards which have hedges.

Walls are colonised by mosses and lichens and are more attractive if left to these velvety plants. Lichens are grey, white and yellow patches of fungus which lives in partnership with algae. The algae produce food from water and carbon dioxide by photosynthesis and then that is absorbed by the fungus. This is a very slow-growing life form, taking two years to reach just one millimetre. It does not like to be disturbed which is why it flourishes on tombstones and church walls. Different sorts of lichen grow depending on the amount of sunlight, the type and texture of stone or animal-droppings on any given surface. It is common to find over 100 different species of the plant in a churchyard. Trees are less attractive hosts to lichens because the acidity of their bark inhibits growth.

Ivy will damage stonework when its roots eat into the surface. A profusion of the plant usually indicates neglect. The chest tombs at St Mary's, Chepstow, are entirely blanketed in this foliage, giving them a cinematic, Gothic appearance. Ivy on graves ought to be severed at ground level and removed when it has died off. Ivy will kill yews but not other species of tree and it does afford nesting birds with an evergreen home. Once sacred to Bacchus and Osiris, ivy is now of particular interest to Christians. It formed the 'corruptible crown' – so called because it did not last – mentioned in I Corinthians, chapter 9 verse 25. Competitors in the Isthmian Games competed for these ivy garlands, and St Paul was reminding them of its transient nature compared to the 'incorruptible crown' waiting for them in heaven.

Among the dappled gravestones and grasses, you will find insects, birds and some creatures that regard the area as a short cut to woods and orchards. We disturbed a fox at Llanwynno and were probably observed by rabbits, bats and weasels as we crossed this living landscape in our unending search for epitaphs. Toy windmills are put on the graves in some cemeteries, such as Thornhill, Cardiff, to discourage the rabbits. We heard of one Minister who used to interrupt meetings occasionally to observe the badgers.

Bats are associated with horror stories. However, old tales of blood-sucking vampires and traumatic accounts of having these furry characters tangled up in your hair are well off the mark. They are a protected species that feasts on insects and they prefer to stay well clear of humans. Greater Horseshoe bats, so called because of the horseshoe shape of their nose, and Long-eared bats like high roof spaces in churches, but their droppings make them unpopular with those who look after these buildings.

Guto Nyth Brân's gravestone at Llanwynno (see Chapter Eight).

Pipistrelles actually look for cracks in stone and tiled areas in which to make their homes. Many churchyard bats use porches as feeding-posts during the night, returning to higher roosts and breeding-colonies during the day.

Butterflies, especially the Holly Blue, enjoy graveyards. It feasts on ivy and holly and lays its eggs on both plants in turn. The Speckled Wood likes the darker parts of a churchyard where the trees offer some shade to grasses. The Wall Brown prefers tall grasses by a gravestone. Butterflies that we see in our gardens, like Red Admirals, are attracted by the purple-flowering buddleia and will seek out nettles to feed their larvae on.

Although the yew is the most widely-known churchyard tree, many other species are found within God's Acre: beech, sweet chestnut, ash, hawthorn, oak, horse chestnut, lime and ornamental trees such as the cherry. The hawthorn or May tree was very important to the Celts. It was always the tree of the 'little people' and, in folklore, it was unwise to cut one down.

Yew-trees have been referred to as the sentinels over the graves of our ancestors. Some are so old as to have sheltered monks and other holy men before churches or monasteries were even built.

There are famous examples of yew-trees throughout Wales. The bleeding yew at Nevern is thought to represent Christ's wounds on the cross. A blood-like liquid oozes from a gash in the bark about five feet from the ground. Some say that it is the sap from a fungal-infected wound, while others think it may be a breakdown of the heartwood of the tree. Another answer is that it is rain water trapped in the reddish bark that emerges tinted by it. Nationalists claim that it will weep until a Welshman occupies the local castle again.

One of the reasons that these trees are regarded with great interest is their fantastic age. Some have girths approaching 25 feet, which makes them 1500 years old. A tree with a girth of 30 feet will be 2500 years old. Llanfoist has a 33-foot specimen. Growth slows down with age and may even stop for centuries but even a yew with a ten-foot girth will have been around over 300 years. At Llandegai there is a whole avenue of yews leading up to the church but behind it is a massive example which must be a thousand years old.

The yew had significance in pre-Christian times. It was thought to have magical properties. Wands were made of the wood and so were diviners' rods. They were Pagan symbols of immortality and were planted beside Bronze Age barrows before they appeared in churchyards.

The Book of Llandaf stated that, 'between the yew tree and church door' sanctuary was available for those who sought it. In the fourteenth century, a royal edict demanded that yews must be planted in all churchyards to protect the buildings from strong winds.

On Palm Sunday when palms were unobtainable, pussy willow was often used as a substitute but so were yew branches. The evergreen foliage of yews

An ancient yew-tree at St Michael's – as old as the medieval graves there.

provided a carpet of green to offer decoration during the religious celebrations. In Ireland the custom persists and yews there are still known as palms today.

Popular opinion has it that the planting of yews was for obtaining material for bow makers. They were the national weapon of defence in Wales, made famous by the archers at Agincourt. Shakespeare referred to it as the 'double fatal yew', being used in the making of a weapon and because of its poisonous qualities. One authority derived the word Yeomen from Yewmen, that is, those who used yew-bows. The slowness of growth and the smallness of their numbers in churchyards suggest that only a minute proportion of the bows required by archers could have been yielded by church yews.

Welsh and indeed British yews did not produce the finest bows. Imported yew, especially from Spain, was used in the best workshops. Even in Medieval times there was a lively trade with continental Europe for all sorts of goods. Specialist dealers would acquire the necessary material, transport it throughout the countryside and sell it on to craftsmen. Spanish yew cost three times as much as British yew. In any case the most popular wood for Welsh archers was elm. Price and performance were as much a part of the equation then as now.

Keeping beasts away from sacred ground was also a matter of concern. Cattle and horses could easily damage graveyards and nobody wanted to find stray animals stuck knee-deep in the earth reserved for departed loved ones. The foliage of yews is lethal to grazing creatures so it certainly helped to protect churchyards from wandering domestic animals. It was also a crude form of fencing.

Though Shakespeare regarded the yew as a dismal tree, 'Cheerless, unsocial plant that loves to dwell midst skulls and coffins, epitaphs and worms', it has also been seen in a very different light. Between the sixth and tenth century, the yew's great longevity made it a symbol of immortality and an emblem of resurrection because of its verdant appearance.

Whatever their true purpose, yew-trees are an integral part of many burial grounds. They add colour and shape and without them the character of these churchyards would be very different.

Chapter Eleven

Funeral Folklore of Wales

The more important an event is in the cycle of human life, the more likely it is to be wrapped in folklore, myth and legend. Because death has such a traumatic impact on those who witness it, and causes such deep grief and sorrow to the loved ones and friends who are bereaved, it attracts massive amounts of folklore.

One of the most striking of these is the *Canwyll Corff* (Corpse Candle). Some legends connect the corpse candle with St David in the fifth century. He is said to have prayed earnestly that the people that he loved and among whom he had carried out his Christian work should be given some warning indication to help them to prepare for death. The legend maintains that St David had a vision in which he was informed that his prayer was answered and the Welsh people whom he loved would never again die unprepared. Before their earthly life ended, the people in St David's land would see a dim light – like the light of a taper – whenever and wherever death was imminent. Unaccountably, reports of these ghostly lights come more often from South Wales than the rest of the country.

These corpse candles are said to come out of the mouth of the person who is to die and travel to the graveyard and hover over the site of the grave. In Aberglasney, a servant girl saw five of these lights come out of a bedroom where five other servant girls were sleeping. In the morning they were found dead. The room had been whitewashed and it is possible that fumes from the walls in a small, crowded bedroom killed them all. (The pianist and entertainer, Liberace, almost died when fumes of cleaning fluid used on his elaborate suits affected him during the night!)

George Henry Borrow, in his book *Wild Wales*, recorded that corpse candles are seen a few nights before death. For

George Borrow: adventurer and author.

example, that of a tinker was observed before he was drowned in a flash flood at a ford. There was also a report that three corpse candles were seen by several people going down a river. Shortly afterwards three men were drowned.

Among the other stories which Borrow recorded was one of a man returning from market in Llaneglwys to Llangurig, not far from Pumlumon. The essence of this account was that the corpse candle itself was no mere warning but was capable of inflicting fatal damage on anyone who touched it. The weather was very bad with rain and wind blowing savagely in the traveller's face. No normal candle flame could have withstood such conditions, but he could neither see the corpse candle nor avoid it. As it touched him, he was struck dead. Borrow's informant went on to exonerate the candle from any malevolent intention against the traveller. It was simply on its way to foretell the death of a local woman whose husband was a wool dealer, and she, according to the story, was dead in less than a fortnight.

Accidents on mountains or steep-sided valleys, tragedies from land or sea, had a particular association with corpse candles. Where a ship met its death on the rocks, or a coach overturned and killed the occupants, clusters of corpse candles would be seen. Some folklorists have suggested that witnesses to supposed corpse candles are actually reporting 'will-o-the-wisps' – travelling lights thought to be created by marsh gas. But this theory cannot account for all corpse candles. Especially when you consider that these sinister lights have sometimes been witnessed inside a room.

Not merely balls or cylinders of light, corpse candles were sometimes seen as lighted skulls; others bore a strange resemblance – like a soft-focus photograph – to the person who was about to die. In some accounts the lights varied in size and luminosity; and this also seemed to relate to the person who was about to die. A very small infant would be represented by a tiny candle, a young child by a bigger area of light. The colour of the flame has been described by witnesses as 'sulphurous blue'; although it has also been recorded that the light changes colour to indicate male or female corpses.

Despite their insubstantial and ephemeral appearance, corpse candles are said to be remarkably powerful. One witness reported that his father, when coming into contact with one, had been flung from his horse. It is also noted in the folklore that the corpse candle seems to trace the movement of the corpse itself – *before that movement actually takes place!* If the candle pauses in its path, the bearers carrying the corpse will do so at the same spot. If the candle moves aside, as though to let someone pass, the bearers of the coffin will do the same. On those doubly sad occasions where two candles meet, the funerals they presage will do the same. A common denominator in all corpse-candle folklore is that they should be avoided, but if an observer looks back along the route which the corpse candle has taken, that observer will allegedly see the deceased, the bearers and mourners.

Some people are reported to have seen complete phantom funerals: the hearse, coffin and bearers, mourners and bystanders would all be visible. Such a phantom funeral is known as a Toili – and it was thought that there was a danger of being swept up by it and carried to the same fate as the corpse! Funerals, in the days when they were frequently reported, tended to be very formal occasions, and, as such, represented the dead person's popularity and social status.

Once again Borrow is our informant. He tells how the 'Welsh Shakespeare', Twm o'r Nant (Thomas Edwards), was born in a dingle at a place called Pen Porchell in the vale of Clwyd which was on the Estate of Iolo Goch the poet. Under an old portrait of Tom is written:

> Llun Gŵr yw Llawn gwir Awen;
> Y Byd a lanwodd o'i Ben.

Or translated:

> God in his head the Muse instill'd,
> And from his head the world he fill'd.

Tom was a carter by trade but he had kept a tollgate in South Wales for two years. He explained that he gave it up because he became weary of the phantoms that would pass through the shut gate at midnight without paying. He claimed to have seen ghosts, goblins and many phantom hearses.

Yet another fascinating story recorded by Borrow concerned a different type of advanced information, or premonition, of death. In Borrow's account this took the form of supernatural knocking. A woman and her husband were disturbed by the sound of a horse and a voice outside the house for three nights running. But when they went to look for the source of the disturbance, there was nothing to be seen. Then came the news that the woman's sister had died in childbirth and that her twin babies were also dead.

Wakes used to be a widespread funeral custom in Wales. Although some were sombre, others were relatively merry affairs with smoking, food, drink and games, in some of which the corpse was a participant. It was felt important to keep the mourners well fed and watered both before and after a funeral. Warm ale and cold ale were served. Some researchers have suggested that cheerful celebrations, including the enjoyment of food and drink, served as a psychic defence against the presence of death.

A verse of Betjeman's refers to the ale-drinking practice:

> 'Twas thus the village drunk its beer
> With its relations buried near
> And that is why we often see
> Inns where the alehouse used to be
> Close to the church where prayers were said
> And Masses for the village dead.

The custom of sin-eating is based on the belief that the past misdemeanours of the deceased could be absorbed by using the coffin lid as a resting place for food which was then consumed by the Parish sin-eater. Relatives and friends, or the Parish itself, would pay for this food – and a poor man, to whom starvation was a more immediate threat than anything supernatural, would be paid to eat the food which had absorbed the sins of the departed. Unlike the dead person, the sin-eater could then repent and be absolved. The idea was that he would become a type of scapegoat and take on the sins of the deceased. This sin-eating custom was well known in the Welsh borders, but historian and folklorist, Catrin Stevens's research has revealed examples in West Wales. In Mary Webb's novel, *Precious Bane,* there is an account of a young man, Gideon, who undertakes the role of sin-eater for his deceased father. The custom even travelled to the New World with Welsh immigrants.

Apart from sin-eating, there were other ways of trying to avoid unwelcome consequences in the afterlife. The devil was said to lurk in dark corners, ready to spring out and trap the soul of an unwary sinner, so the designers of the oldest graveyards tended to favour circular burial grounds – like the example at

Circular graveyard at Penbryn.

Penbryn – where there were no corners in which Satan could hide. The belief that the devil had a preference for dark, shadowy places, where the unprepared could be taken by surprise, is also reflected in the preference for graves on the sunny, southern side of a church. The shady, northern plots were filled last.

In medieval Wales, the Sexton, or grave-digger, was seen as a type of medicine man. It was thought that, if you took a handful of the consecrated churchyard soil which he dug, it would protect you from black magic. The handful of soil was normally sprinkled over the head as a psychic disinfectant! The Sexton would later hold out his spade, and mourners would put money on it to help to pay for the funeral. Many people were so poor that they needed such help from their neighbours to cover their burial costs.

Sometimes, on the morning of a burial a sinister visitor came bearing a measuring rod called a 'fey'. This rod, made of aspen and carved with ogham letters and symbols, was used to measure the deceased to ensure a proper fit within the final resting-place. The mourners would avert their eyes from this rod in awe and terror – because it was thought that if this rod caught your measure, your death was inevitable.

In Ireland they have the *banshee* who will wail and come for the person who is to die or who is already dead. The Welsh version is the *Gwrach-y-rhibyn*. One was reported regularly at Caerphilly castle and would appear as a Green Lady. This Green Lady would flit from turret to turret so openly that one night some of the town boys nearly caught her. In contrast to others of her kind, she seems to have been a benign spirit, with no bad intent, and one who actually enjoyed the chase!

The uncanny hooting of owls, swooping over midnight graveyards on their silent wings, accounts for the sinister legends of supernatural, owl-like entities. Welsh legends of the graveyard screech-owl bear an uncanny similarity to the Middle Eastern myths about Lilith. In that ancient legend, she was a demoness, the first wife of Adam, before Eve was created. On her wedding night, Lilith was so shocked and repelled by Adam's keen interest in sex, that she uttered a shrill scream and flew away from him, never to return to the conjugal bed. As time passed, Eve replaced her and had the children that Lilith could never have. In bitter hatred and jealousy, Lilith, the screech-owl, otherwise known as a night-haunting vampire, attacked young children as they slept. The Welsh versions of the screech-owl legends maintained that the owls were harbingers of doom – and that if they were seen visiting a house, a death would occur there.

Grave Humour & Unusual Epitaphs from beyond Wales

For all its morbidity, the graveyard has always been a source of great creativity and entertainment. This means that the profound and the amusing have often kept company in epitaphs and memorials.

How else could you explain that the most commonly used couplet

As I am now, so you must be,
Therefore prepare to follow me.

is followed in one valleys churchyard by the following witticism?

To follow you I'm not content
Until I know which way you went

And as the next list demonstrates, this fascination with death's black humour isn't the sole preserve of the Welsh. It is found the world over, in all walks of life.

ACTORS AND ARTISTS

WALLACE BEERY . . . Actor

No man is Indispensable
But some are Irreplaceable

CONSTANCE BENNETT . . . Actress

Do not disturb.

MEL BLANC . . . Voice of Bugs Bunny & other Cartoon Greats

That's All Folks

W. C. Fields . . . Comedian

On the whole, I'd rather be in Philadelphia

John Gay . . . Playwright & Composer

Life is a jest, and all thing shew it
I thought so once, and now I know it

Oscar Wilde . . . Playwright & Wit

Either this wallpaper goes – or I do!

BARMAIDS AND WIVES

ANN COLLINS . . . Barmaid

'T was as she tript from cask to cask,
In a bung-hole she quickly fell,
Suffocation was her task,
She had no time to say farewell.

A WIFE . . . Llanelly, Gwent

This spot's the sweetest
I've seen in my life
For it raises my flowers
And covers my wife.

COWBOYS AND GANGSTERS

ALPHONSE CAPONE . . . Tax Evader

My Jesus Mercy

ANONYMOUS AND INEPT GUNSLINGER . . . Cripple Creek

He called Bill Smith
a lier (sic)

LESTER MOORE . . . Boot Hill Cowboy, Tombstone, Arizona

Here lies Lester Moore
Four slugs from a 44
No Les no More.

HOG SLAUGHTERERS

JOHN HIGGS . . . Pig Killer

Here lies John Higgs
A famous man for killing pigs.
For killing pigs was his delight
Both morning, afternoon and night.
Both cold and heat he did endure
Which no Physician could cure.
His knife is laid his work is done
I hope to heaven his soul is gone.

SOLDIERS AND STRONGMEN

ALEXANDER THE GREAT . . . Conqueror

> A tomb now suffices for him
> For whom the world was not enough

CAPTAIN BUTLER . . . Soldier

> Sacred to the memory of Captain Maurice James Butler,
> Royal Irish Rifles
> Accidently shot by his Batman on The Fourth Day
> Of
> April 1882
> "Well Done Thou Good And Faithful Servant"

SAMSON . . . Judge of Israel, Strongman & Temple Demolisher

> Let me die with the Philistines!

INDEX OF GRAVE LOCATIONS FOR TALKING STONES

Acknowledgements

Mid Wales
Julian Williams
David Petley-Jones
Ronald Morris
Marjorie Worthington
Liz Pitman
Dr Russell Davies

South East Wales
Dr Bill Jones
Major Martin Everett
Glyn Jenkins
Richard J. Brewer

West Wales
Ken Jones
Sian Rhiannon Williams
John M. O. Jones
Catrin Stevens

North Wales
Rev John Gilliebrands
Gareth Wood
Buddug Medi
J. Elwyn Hughes
Rob Piercey

Cardiff to Merthyr
Anthony Jenkins
Keith Chadwick
Ann Flint
Mario Basini
Aaron Jones

Western Valleys to Carmarthen
Stan Pope
Dean Wyn Evans
Peter Stead
Sian Owen
Alan Richards

The Church in Wales for access to locations featured in the book

All **location photographs** by Richard Pawelko, except for the one on page 45 which is courtesy of the West Glamorgan Archive Service.

Select Bibliography

Chris Barber *Mysterious Wales* Blorenge Books
George Borrow *Wild Wales* T. Nelson & Sons, Ltd
Brian Kemp *Church Monuments* Shire Publications
Hilary Lees *English Churchyard Memorials* Tempus
Alun Roberts *Discovering Welsh Graves* University of Wales Press
David M. Wilson *Awful Ends* British Museum Press
Western Mail